DORSET PIONEERS

DORSET PIONEERS

Jack Dwyer

The
History
Press

Front cover: 'Sea Venture and Consorts at Sea' by Deryck Foster. Admiral George Somers, on a voyage to relieve Sir Walter Raleigh's colonists, discovered Bermuda.

Deryck Foster was born in 1924 in Bournemouth, a seaside resort now in the county of Dorset. He studied at Bournemouth's Southern School of Art, now The Arts University College, Bournemouth.

Deryck Foster is one of those rare marine artists whose skill as a painter of sea and sail is paralleled by experience as a watch officer aboard Britain's sail training schooners, the *Sir William Churchill* and the *Malcolm Miller*, and several years as a bowman of the Royal National Lifeboat Institutions Yarmouth Lifeboat, based on the Isle of Wight.

Deryck Foster's paintings are in the permanent collection of the Russell Coates Art Gallery, Bournemouth and the National Maritime Museum, Greenwich, England.

www.visit-dorset.com

First published 2009

The History Press
The Mill, Brimscombe Port
Stroud, Gloucestershire, GL5 2QG
www.thehistorypress.co.uk

© Jack Dwyer, 2009

The right of Jack Dwyer to be identified as the Author
of this work has been asserted in accordance with the
Copyrights, Designs and Patents Act 1988.

ISBN 978 0 7524 5346 0

Typesetting and origination by The History Press
Printed in Great Britain

Contents

Acknowledgements

Without the help and encouragement of my wife Doreen and especially my son Adrian, this timid book would not have appeared. So my warmest thanks go to them.

I am also greatly indebted to: Laura All, Senior Commissioning Editor, The History Press, USA www.historypress.net; Mike Andrews, Christchurch Local History Society, Dorset, England; Ed and Byron Blackmore, Thomas Howe Demonstration Forest Foundation, Canada; Lord Edward and Lady Dione Digby www.minterne.co.uk; Keith Forbes, www.bermuda-online.org; Roberta Goldstein, Communications Manager, The Thomas Coram Foundation www.coram.org; Lt-Col. David Hamilton, The Institution of Royal Engineers, Chatham, www.instre.org; Clifford Harper; Charlotte Hughes, Assistant Curator, Royal Engineers Museum and Library, Chatham, England www.remuseum.org.uk; David Lang , Director and Secretary, Bank of Bermuda Foundation, Bermuda www.bankofbermuda.com; Fran and Gordon Lee; Norman MacKay, Dorset Heritage Museum, Ontario, Canada www.dorsetheritagemuseum. ca; Deborah Padgett, Media Relations Manager, Jamestown-Yorktown Foundation, Virginia, USA www.historyisfun.org; Lisa Peppan, webmaster, The Columbia Detachment of the Royal Engineers, Canada www.royalengineers.ca; Janet Pickering, Manager of the Tolpuddle Martyrs' Museum and Festival, Dorset, England; www. tolpuddlemartyrs.org.uk; Judith Pothecary, Lyme Regis Twinning Association, England; John Raymond, The High Sheriff of Dorset; Rollo Reid, Technical Director, Reid Steel, Christchurch, Dorset www.reidsteel.com; Rob Sanders, TUC Senior Publishing Officer www.tuc.org.uk; Ann Simon, Tourism Manager, Christchurch Borough Council; Ann Smith, Archivist for Sherborne Castle and Minterne House, Dorset www.sherbornecastle.com; Steve Spring, GIS Manager, Dorset County Council; Sheryl Stanton, Curator, Admiral Digby Museum, Digby, Canada www. admuseum.ns.ca; Elena Strong, Acting Curator of the Bermuda Maritime Museum www.bmm.bm; Lars Tharp and Alison Duke of The Foundling Museum, London www.foundlingmuseum.org.uk; Susan Twist, Yukon Archives, Government of Yukon, Canada www.tc.gov.yk.ca; Duncan Walker, Collections Officer, Russell-Cotes Art Gallery and Museum, Bournemouth; www.russell-cotes.bournemouth.gov.uk; David Walsh, Economic Development Manager, Dorset County Council www.dorsetforyou. com; David Watkins, Service and Operations Manager, Poole Museum Service www. boroughofpoole.com; Timothy Watkins, Norquist Watkins, Barristers & Solicitors and Royal Engineers Living History Group in British Columbia www.royalengineers. ca; Teressa Williams, Museum Librarian, Anchorage Museum, Library and Archives www.anchoragemuseum.org; Peter Woodward, Curator of Dorset County Museum and Val Davies, Dorchester, England www.dorsetcountymuseum.org.

Finally, this book would not have reached the bookshelves without the support, guidance, and not inconsiderable patience, of Nicola Guy, Commissioning Editor, and the rest of the team at The History Press Ltd.

Introduction

Far from the ancient towns and castles of the English county where I live is another Dorset in North America. The small community lies deep among the forests and lakes of Central Ontario, and when some Canadian friends took my wife and me there some years ago, it set me on a trail discovering the astonishing number of places elsewhere in the vast North American continent with historic links of one sort or another with the English county. I found that Dorset people are concerned in one way or another with the founding of eight US states: the Virginias, Maryland, the Carolinas, Georgia, Maine and Massachusetts, places as far apart as Texas, New York, Vermont, and Yukon, and with four Canadian provinces: British Columbia, Newfoundland, and Nova Scotia, as well as Ontario.

Perhaps the best known of all these people is the founder of Virginia, Walter Raleigh, who lorded over a Dorset castle, but through this book I tell of other Dorset folk who have played what might be called interesting, and even important, roles in the story of North America.

George Washington, yes, the first President of the United States...I have seen no evidence that he had ever been to Dorset, but there are family connections with the great man, and they are revealed in the tiny village of Steeple and its ancient church which, incidentally, lacks a steeple. A coat of arms engraved in stone in the porch, and another painted in scarlet on the roof interior, are precisely the same as the coat of arms on Washington's signet ring which shows stars and stripes. It could almost be the original pattern for the American flag; the Washington arms is quartered with those of the squires of Steeple village, the Lawrence family, which is allied with the Washingtons by the marriage of one of its sons, Edmund Lawrence, to Agnes de Wessington in 1390. Fanciful, perhaps, but what is undeniable is that the flag of the US capital hangs proudly inside the fifteenth-century church. It was presented by a former mayor of Washington during a visit some years ago.

So did the connection between America and Dorset begin in the fourteenth century? Absurd, of course, because 200 years passed before the English set foot on the North American continent in an expedition funded by one Walter Raleigh, who figures in the first two chapters of this book. Succeeding chapters tell of other folk from all walks of Dorset life who have played an active role in linking the county with North America. There is, for instance, Admiral Sir George Somers

(Chapter 2), son of a Lyme Regis shopkeeper, who by his courageous action at sea saved the first English settlement in North America from starvation. There was the Reverend John White (Chapter 3), the Dorchester vicar who supported the pilgrim founders of Massachusetts, and Robert Gorges (Chapter 4), who did the same in Maine. The second Lord Baltimore (Chapter 5) added Maryland to the growing British Empire, and the barons Ashley and Clarendon shared ownership of Carolina (Chapter 6). John Ridout (Chapter 7) became secretary to the Maryland governor and a member of the Upper Assembly.

Rear-Admiral Robert Digby (Chapter 8) of Minterne Magna was in command of the North American fleet when the United States won its independence and British rule was confirmed in Canada. His ships escorted thousands of refugees who fled from the new republic to Nova Scotia, where a town was renamed Digby in his honour.

Another sailor who won a battle of a different kind was Thomas Coram (Chapter 9), a Lyme Regis seafarer who became a shipbuilder and later succeeded in raising the funds to build a world-famous hostel for foundlings (destitute young children) in London.

The sea, and the fish within it, lies behind the official twinning with Newfoundland and the warm relationship which thrives between the two (Chapter 10).

I

In Quest of El Dorado

On a hill overlooking Sherborne, Sir Walter Raleigh was so enchanted by the view of the lush countryside and the picturesque abbey and castle in the valley of the River Yeo that he tumbled from his horse and, in the words of a contemporary, 'ploughed up the earth where he fell'. One can imagine the favourite of Queen Elizabeth I scrambling to his feet and picking clods of Dorset from his manicured beard while his riding companion, Sir Adrian Gilbert, laughs and quips that his stepbrother had 'taken physical seizure of the land he coveted'. Sir John Harrington's account of how his fellow courtier had fallen for the ancient manor may be a little imaginative, but Raleigh did conceive a strong desire for it on his journeys between London and the West Country. His wish was eventually granted by his beloved queen, not least for bringing her England's first colony, which he named Virginia after her vaunted virginity. By becoming Lord of the Manor and the most famous resident of Sherborne, Raleigh forged the first and best-known link between the English county of Dorset and North America.

Although history credits him with settling Virginia, he never set foot on it. He had attempted to sail to the New World in his early twenties when he joined an expeditionary fleet of seven ships commanded by one of his three half-brothers, Sir Humphrey Gilbert. In 1578 England was still on the starting block in the race for colonies, while Spain and Portugal were firmly entrenched in both Americas and returning their treasure ships to Europe low in the water. England had neglected the opportunity given it in 1497 when John Cabot erected the English flag on Newfoundland and claimed the island for Henry VII, only five years after Columbus discovered the Caribbean. The picture changed with the rise of English nationalism, Henry VIII's breach with Rome, and the ambitious rule of his daughter, Elizabeth, when, in the words of her chancellor Sir Francis Bacon, it became a patriotic duty 'to singe the King of Spain's beard'. So, as well as a Royal warrant to start putting pink on the global map, Gilbert was armed with plenty of cannon to singe a few galleons while he was about it.

Seagoing ventures of this kind were a matter of private enterprise in Elizabeth's time, and she had a piece of the action with her own 100 ton *Falcon*, which she entrusted to the command of young Raleigh. He was looking forward eagerly to the excitement, but unfortunately the expedition never got far from Devon.

Violent storms forced the captains to return, except for the impulsive Raleigh who pressed on only to fall foul of a Spanish flotilla. Many of his crew were killed or wounded in the ensuing skirmish, but he managed to nurse the battered *Falcon* back to Dartmouth.

In the years that followed he was engaged in many a bloody adventure at sea and on land as England strove to become a great European power. His exploits took him twice to the other side of the Atlantic, but they were to South America and the Caribbean looking for treasure. The three expeditions he funded to settle North America under a Royal patent granted in 1584 went without him, and by the time the last of them succeeded, he was losing his colonising zeal and likely to lose his head; he was languishing in the Tower of London under sentence of death.

Raleigh was born around 1552 at Hayes Barton in the south of Devon, Dorset's neighbouring county, to the first of three wives of a gentleman farmer, who might have been the Walter Rawley who represented the parliamentary constituency of Wareham in Dorset at one time. The boy's mother, Katherine, was a member of the Drake family, the widow of a Gilbert, and related through marriage to those other West Country buccaneers, Grenville and Carew, and so naturally the sea coursed through Raleigh's veins. Sir John Millais' famous painting *The Boyhood of Raleigh* shows the lad listening enraptured to the yarns of a grizzled mariner on a Devon shore. His youthful years are vague in detail, but he is known to have been brought up in the Protestant tradition. After four years studying at Oxford he fought with the Huguenots against the Catholic armies in France, perhaps influenced by the fact that his maternal grandfather was an exiled French Huguenot, Sir Philip Champernowne.

During the Irish rebellion against Elizabeth's stern repression, he was commissioned a captain in 1580 and led the attack on Smerwick Castle in County Kerry. Six hundred Spanish and Italian mercenaries who surrendered on the promise of safe conduct were massacred. For this 'glorious' military excess, Raleigh was rewarded with the Munster estate forfeited from the rebel leader, the Earl of Desmond, and on it he settled a colony of 300-400 Englishmen, mostly from Dorset and the adjacent counties of Devon and Somerset. He left behind him in Ireland a fearsome military reputation and an illegitimate daughter, Alice Goold, whom he later married off to a nobleman in the Channel Islands and remembered financially in his will.

While in Ireland he met another beneficiary of Desmond's confiscated land, the poet Edmund Spenser, who held various appointments for the queen. Spenser showed Raleigh his monumental work, *The Faërie Queene,* a moralising fiction of twelve chivalrous knights who defend truth against falsehood on behalf of Gloriana – Good Queen Bess, of course. Raleigh, a gifted writer himself, instantly recognised a dramatic advance in English poetry, the first really great verse in the language since Chaucer's *Canterbury Tales,* and on his recommendation the six volumes were published. They became an instant success and influenced the greatest English poets, from Shakespeare to Keats and Byron.

Raleigh could have been a clone for one of Spenser's bold knights, being tall, dark and handsome with a lofty bearing, except that he was proud and vain to the point of arrogance, merciless in arms, and greedy for wealth. Notwithstanding his faults, his dashing intelligence and command of the necessary art of flattery rapidly elevated him in the royal esteem, and he was admitted to court. One royal favour followed another in the 1580s and into the 1590s: a knightly touch on the shoulder in January 1585, Lord Wardenship of the Stannaries, which gave him a nice commission on Cornish tin, Lord Lieutenant-Governor of Cornwall, Admiral of the West, and the lucrative patent for wine vendors' licences. Meanwhile, his rising influence with the queen was provoking jealousy and suspicion among her fawning courtiers and contributed to his eventual downfall.

In 1583 Humphrey Gilbert hoist sail for North America, once again aiming to locate the elusive north-west passage that would open the door to the seductive prizes of the Orient. Gilbert raised the English flag over Newfoundland and left some settlers, but they were never seen again, and he perished in a storm at sea on his way home. Raleigh had hoped to sail with Gilbert in command of his own vessel, the 200 ton *Bark Raleigh*, but Elizabeth wanted him at home. In 1584 she reassigned Gilbert's patent to Raleigh, who favoured the more southern territories that were destined to become the US states of Virginia, Maryland and the Carolinas.

The patent holder was commanded 'to discover out, searche, find out and view such heathen and barbarous lands, countries and territories not actually possessed of any Christian prince nor inhabited by Christian people'. The reference to 'any Christian prince' and his possessions may have been a coded warning to her ambitious lieutenant not to annoy her maritime rival, the Catholic King of Spain, or at least not too much, for it was a delicate moment in the wily queen's diplomacy to keep her realm at peace with Spain while it suited England.

She obliged Raleigh, now extremely rich, to stay in England at the time of his three expeditions to settle Virginia, which then denoted the whole of the Atlantic coast from Florida to Newfoundland. The first, a promising reconnaissance by two ships, encouraged a second voyage that left 100 men on an island, Roanoke, offered by an Indian chief off the shore of North Carolina. The men watching the sails disappear over the horizon were not of the colonising mould, however, and when Francis Drake sailed that way he found them in some distress and brought them home. A third attempt, two years later, to establish a settlement in Chesapeake Bay to the north of the Carolinas boded better, for it included women and children, but sadly the 117 vanished without trace. Twenty years were to pass before a lasting occupation was achieved, when three ships penetrated the Chesapeake, dropped anchor in the James River, and established Jamestown. They had been sent by the London Company, a joint stock enterprise to which Raleigh, as a partner, had assigned the Royal patent, reserving to himself a fifth of any gold and silver found.

The three unsuccessful gambles had cost Raleigh £40,000, an enormous sum by modern standards, but the setback to his fortunes was temporary, and he remained a wealthy man, for his own privateers continued to lighten Iberian ships of precious stones and metals, spices, sugar and other rich plunder. In 1585 he had put money into Drake's expedition, the one that rescued the 100 unhappy settlers on Roanoke and whose twenty-nine vessels and 2,300 soldiers and sailors created mayhem in the Caribbean, capturing six prizes and greatly enriching the investors. The queen was grateful for Spain's unwitting contribution to her exchequer and smiled on Raleigh with further benevolence. She appointed him captain of the guard responsible for her personal security and also governor of the fort on Portland Bill on the Dorset coast, even though his supremacy in her affections was being challenged by the advent at court of an ambitious young aristocrat, the second Earl of Essex. The rivalry between the two continued on and off until Elizabeth suspected Essex of plotting armed rebellion and removed his handsome head in 1601.

Raleigh was now among the queen's closest, staunchest and most favoured advisers, ever-present as she intrigued to make post-Reformation England a power to be reckoned with in Europe. He teased her vanity with eulogies of her sovereign being, impressed her high intelligence with his wit, and supported her expansionist ambitions. He had brought her the firstborn of an empire that would one day cover a quarter of the globe, and she appointed him Lord and Governor of Virginia, but kept him back from foreign excursions because she wanted his dependability close to her side. One of his poems laments:

> To seek new worlds for gold, for praise, for glory,
> To try desire, to try love, severed far,
> When I was gone she sent her memory
> More strongly than were ten thousand ships of war
> To call me back.

When Spain threatened invasion, Elizabeth appointed her faithful lieutenant to her War Council with the duty to prepare the country's shore defence, and he pressed for heavy cannon to strengthen the fortifications at Portland and the nearby port of Weymouth. In 1588 a formidable armada with 130 war galleons, thirty smaller ships, 30,000 soldiers and sailors, 2,000 slaves and nearly 4,000 guns was sighted off the Dorset coast and engaged by Lord Howard's puny fleet. The lumbering galleons were no match for Howard's light and agile ships and one after another were destroyed or captured. The English gave them no peace and continued to harass them as they fled up the North Sea to disaster on the stormy rocks of Scotland and Ireland. Out of the 160 or so vessels that set out from Spain, only fifty-four survived and sailed home. Raleigh had not been allowed to join the battle - much to his disappointment, no doubt - but he let the money-starved Treasury have his year-old flagship *Ark Royal* in exchange for an 'IOU' for £5,000, and it led the English fleet to the attack.

His remarkable career reached its zenith in 1592 when Elizabeth granted the prize so close to his heart. She 'persuaded' the bishop of Bath and Wells to lease the church-owned Sherborne Manor to Raleigh at a rental cost of £360 a year, and he thanked her with a £250 jewel of unknown provenance. Sherborne meant far more to him than just another desirable acquisition, and was a convenient halt on his travels between the western ports and the capital. He described Sherborne in his poetry as his 'fortune's fold', the tranquil enclosure of his private life and domestic happiness away from the sea and the equally inconstant affairs of state in London.

Here in one of the most delightful areas of south-west England, deep in rich farming land and surrounded by woods and hills that were alive with sport at that time, he could act the comfortable role of gentleman landowner, running and improving the estate, and engaging in the social and formal life of Dorset. A cultivated man, studiously interested in history as his later writings were to show, he must have been impressed by Sherborne's past. Here the invading Romans had subjugated the native British, the Saxons buried two of their kings, and the Norman conquerors overlaid the foundations of the Saxon cathedral with one of the finest abbeys in the land.

Six months after the gift of Sherborne, Raleigh was in disgrace. Prophetic hints of his fall can be detected in verse attributed to him, though its authenticity is uncertain. From extolling the virtues of his revered sovereign in affectionate but platonic terms (he was never intimately linked to her to the extent that Essex and the Earl of Leicester were), his poetic effusion became overtly sexual and even soppy, according to Robert Lacey in his absorbing biography, *Sir Walter Raleigh*. Compare the elegant opening to his earlier poem *To the Queen*:

> Our passions are most like to floods and streams;
> The shallow murmur, but the deep are dumb.
> So when affections yield discourse, it seems
> The bottom is but shallow whence they came.
> They that are rich in words must needs discover
> That they are poor in that which makes a lover.

with this doggerel quoted by Lacey:

> Her eyes he would should be of light,
> A violet breath and lips of jelly,
> Her hair not black, not over-bright,
> And of the softest down her belly.

Plainly, a more approachable lady was being addressed. When Elizabeth found out that he had impregnated one of her ladies-in-waiting, her hero was at sea, having sailed from the Cornish port of Falmouth with a fleet in which he had sunk most of his capital and a £10,000 loan. The object was to collect some more Iberian treasure. The queen had shown her confidence with a couple of ships and £3,000 in cash, but now her canny expectation of a generous return on her investment was temporarily dampened by jealous fury at having been deceived by her trusted confidant. She ordered him back, leaving Sir Martin Frobisher in command of the venture. The errant Raleigh was confined to his London home, Durham House, the former palace of the Bishops of Durham on the Thames Embankment, where he had entertained and debated with notable intellects of the day – scientists, mathematicians, theologians and poets such as Christopher Marlowe. Then he and the expectant Betty (Elizabeth) Throckmorton, daughter of the queen's first ambassador to Paris, were locked in the grim Tower of London.

Banishment from court was a bitter blow to Raleigh's self-esteem. In *Farewell to the Court* he laments:

Like truthless dreams, so are my joys expired,
And past return are all my dandled days;
My love misled, and fancy quite retired,
Of all which past, the sorrow only stays.

and concludes:

Whom care forewarns, ere age and winter cold,
To haste me hence, to find my fortune's fold.

The queen's rage relented when Raleigh's ships brought home a captured Spanish vessel, *Madre de Dios*, with a valuable cargo of which she would be the principal beneficiary, and around Christmas time he and Betty (otherwise known as Bess), by now privately married, were allowed to retire to the 'fold' of his wealth and domestic bliss, the Sherborne estate, to live the life of squire and lady in the castle he had admired from afar. In reality it was a massive fortified palace erected by the Norman bishop Roger de Caen while the abbey was being built. Finding that twelfth century comforts were not to his taste, Raleigh had given up trying to modernise the castle and built another, more correctly described as a mansion, on the foundations of Bishop de Caen's hunting lodge on the opposite bank of the Yeo river. In May 1593, Betty gave birth to a son, Walter, who was baptised in the thirteenth-century village church at Lillington, just south of Sherborne. Their firstborn, a son Damerei, had died in infancy in the previous year while his mother was in the Tower.

Raleigh involved himself in the dealings with his many tenants and enjoyed the country pursuits with his landed friends, hawking at times and hunting deer in the grounds of his estate, but he was still restless with the fever of seafaring and the lure of precious metal. Despite his wife's misgivings he sailed in 1594 with a band of cut-throats and five ships he had fitted out at his own expense to look for the fabled city with shining roofs of gold and walls gleaming with gems that was supposed to lurk somewhere in the South American jungle - El Dorado. With a royal commission to trouble the Spaniards a little, he captured San Josef in Trinidad at the mouth of the Orinoco Delta, in today's Venezuela, and explored the river with rowboats for 400 miles. He did not discover the mines that were gilding his dreams, but covered expenses with the loot brought back to England and demonstrated his literary skill with a lauded account of his exploits, *The Discoverie of Guiana*.

The queen was warming towards her errant knight, even though his stubborn pride prevented him saying he was sorry for not telling her he had seduced a member of her retinue without her permission. She appointed him Admiral to lead an attack on the Spanish port of Cadiz, and it was brilliantly successful. He collected a severe leg-wound in the action and many prizes in the Azores on his way back. The loot, being shared with his sovereign, eased their reconciliation but was not enough to re-admit him to court, although he was still heard in the governance of the land. Since 1597 he had represented a Dorset seat in Parliament and waxed rhetorical on foreign policy, social justice and religious freedom. On the last two subjects he was a typical product of the Renaissance, questioning the orthodoxy of the receding Middle Ages and responding to the new waves of thought and culture flowing from the likes of Michelangelo, Galileo, Copernicus and Da Vinci.

His outspoken scepticism in theological arguments had already got him into trouble. In 1594 he had questioned the whereabouts of the soul in man during a dinner table discussion with county friends and the Reverend Ralph Ironside, vicar of Fordington, now a suburb of Dorchester. The argument led to suspicions of atheism, and not for the first time. The Church of England held an official inquiry at Cerne Abbas, which is on the road to Sherborne, but the charge against Raleigh of unorthodoxy, tantamount to treason in those days, was dropped. Only a month later he talked through the night with a Roman Catholic Father, John Cornelius, who had been arrested at Chideock in West Dorset and imprisoned in Dorchester. After displaying his openness of mind on spiritual matters, Raleigh gave the order for the brave priest to be hanged for not being a Protestant, and the corpse was dismembered before the public and displayed around Dorchester. The martyr's head decorated one of the city gates for some years, gruesome evidence that the Renaissance disciple of freedom of thought had done his duty.

The death of the queen in 1603 was the turning point in Raleigh's fortunes. His jealous enemies in high places persuaded her successor, James I (James VI of Scotland), that Raleigh was plotting against him, and despite his eloquent pleading, a court convicted him on a trumped-up charge of treason. He spent the next twelve years in the Bloody Tower with his wife and son, Walter. They lived in some comfort, but his estates were estreated to the Crown and his appointments annulled. Another son, Carew, was born in the prison in 1605.

The news that a permanent settlement in Virginia was finally secured in 1607 will have reached Raleigh in the Tower, but his interest in colonisation was evaporating. He was engrossed in writing his most famous work, *History of the World*. Only one of the intended five volumes was published, reaching the Second Macedonian War in 130 BC, but it was an immediate bestseller and a remarkably daring analysis of crowned tyranny at a time when the current ruler was keeping him in jail. Raleigh actually expressed thanks for his incarceration, otherwise 'I should hardly have had the leisure to have made myself a foole in print'. *History of the World* exerted a profound influence on Cromwell, Milton and other Parliamentarians in the 1640s Civil War, and has come to be admired as a glowing example of Elizabethan scholarship and prose that illustrates the finer side of a complex personality.

He had long been interested in scientific discovery and set up a laboratory in the prison. It is perhaps surprising that a convicted traitor was allowed to experiment with chemicals while the shock of the Gunpowder Plot was still reverberating through the land, but Raleigh enjoyed the security of international fame. He cultivated a herb garden in the prison grounds for medical research, and the reputed efficacy of his potions reached a wide audience, including the queen, Anne of Denmark, who took her ailing son Henry to see her husband's prisoner on a number of occasions, and Raleigh and the young prince became close friends. The royal doctors failed to cure Henry of a fever, so Anne administered one of Raleigh's prescriptions, and the boy seemed to revive, but he died soon afterwards. Henry had tried to intercede with his father to gain Raleigh's release – 'No king but my father would keep such a bird in a cage', he is quoted as saying - but James was unmoved by appeals for clemency.

A gilded carrot dangled before the eyes of the cash-strapped monarch was a different matter, however. When Raleigh told James about El Dorado, he was released on parole in 1616 to search for it again, but was told he must operate without royal backing. The king could do with some Orinoco gold, but he was nervous about offending the Spanish court because he was hoping his son Charles would marry the Infanta, who would bring a considerable dowry with her to England. So he ordered Raleigh not to molest any of his prospective in-laws' possessions overseas, and in order to keep Madrid on side he secretly gave the Spanish ambassador in London all the details of Raleigh's expedition - the ships involved, armaments, ports of call, estimated dates of arrival, and so on. The paroled prisoner got wind of this double-cross and made a private arrangement of his own with the French, who agreed that if the adventure went wrong he could find refuge on their side of the Channel.

At the age of sixty-three, Raleigh was taking his final gamble. With no support from the Crown, he sold property of his own and of his wife, despite her protestations, and raised £10,000 to fund his second search for the elusive city of gold. Disaster struck almost from the beginning. Storms and sickness battered his fleet on the voyage to South America. The stronghold of San Tomes was sacked and burnt in spite of his orders and the promise to the king to respect Spanish property, and Raleigh's headstrong son Walter was killed in the assault.

The ageing explorer failed to find the fabled riches that would release him from imprisonment. Like so many of his contemporaries he had believed the Spanish soldiers tale. 200 years and several expeditions would pass before the German explorer/naturalist Humboldt exposed El Dorado for what it was - a tragic myth.

Raleigh could have sought safety abroad, but he bravely returned to England and almost certain execution. His previous journeys from Plymouth to London had been joyous, but on this, his last, he was a sick and broken man. He had lost his fortune, his cherished home, and his elder son. After spending the night in the manor house at Poyntington village near Sherborne, and before resuming his journey to the scaffold, he looked down at his beloved estate in the Yeo valley and bade farewell to the hunting woods, the pastures, the abbey where he and his family had prayed, and the castles he would never see again. To a companion, he confided, 'All this was mine, and it was taken from me unjustly.'

While the miserable Raleigh awaited the executioner, the future of Sherborne was being decided. At first it had looked as if he would keep possession. The ninety-nine-year lease had been transmuted into freehold in 1599 in the heyday of his career and the title transferred in trust to his son Walter, reserving the income from the estate to himself and his wife. Unfortunately, the clerk making out the legal document had omitted the vital words that young Walter 'shall and will from henceforth stand and be thereof seized', so the property still belonged to Raleigh. Because of that awful lapse, the estate was forfeit to the king who gave it to his son Henry. The Prince of Wales had wanted Raleigh, his friend and mentor, to have it back on his release from prison, but the young man died just a year later.

The twists and turns in the Sherborne saga had still not ended. The king sold the manor to his mincing lover, Robert Carr, the odious Earl of Somerset, who was proposing to marry Lady Essex. Her divorce was opposed by another member of the court, but after her husband was found poisoned the marriage went ahead. The countess and her lover were implicated in the murder but pardoned. Carr had fallen from grace, however, and Sherborne was once more up for sale. Stability was nigh. In 1617 a kinsman of Lady Raleigh came on to the scene. John Digby, the king's ambassador to Spain and later Earl of Bristol, bought the estate from his royal master for £10,000, a bargain price for such a valuable property, but the king owed Digby money. The Crown's right to ownership was upheld by the courts, despite a vigorous campaign by Lady Raleigh, and eventually she waived her claim in return for a grant of £8,000 and £400 a year for herself and her son Carew for life. It turned out to be a good arrangement for Betty because she lived for a further thirty years and reached the age of eighty-two.

A large crowd gathered in Palace Yard on 29 October 1618 to see the nation's hero of many accomplishments - soldier, sailor, coloniser, poet, scientist and licensed pirate - climb on to the scaffold erected outside the prison. In a long speech justifying his actions he turned to Lord Arundel, watching among a group of lords, and asked if it were true that he had kept his word to return to England. Arundel is reported to have shouted, 'So you did - it is true', but did not mention that after his arrival Raleigh had attempted to escape to France. Coolly, Raleigh ran his fingers along the blade of the axe. 'This is sharp medicine,' he joked, 'but it is a sure cure for all diseases.' On the previous evening, he had added two lines to his moving *Epitaph*:

> And from which earth, and grave, and dust,
> The Lord shall raise me up, I trust.

Today his castles contemplate each other across a lake designed by Capability Brown two centuries after Raleigh's death. The older of the two, now a national monument on lease to the government department, English Heritage, was emasculated by Cromwell's forces after the Royalist Digbys resisted a siege in the Civil War, but enough remains to indicate to the visiting public what a fine palace the Norman abbot had created. The newer castle soon became, like Raleigh himself, a part of Sherborne's history. William of Orange stayed there in 1689 on his way from Holland to seize the English crown. Much later, it was used as a military hospital in the First World War and again in the second world conflict, when it was occupied by the American allies preparing for the Normandy invasion. Raleigh had built it as a four-storey tower with mullioned windows to which the Digbys added wings, creating an H-shape that recognises, so it is said, the brief ownership by Prince Henry, Raleigh's friend and ill-fated son of James I. The house, still owned by the Digby family, is open to the public from spring to autumn and makes up for its lack of architectural distinction by virtue of a beautifully-restored interior showing the influences of four centuries. The elaborately-moulded ceiling in the Green Drawing Room bears the Raleigh arms of five lozenges on a shield and the fleur-de-lys. There is further evidence of Raleigh's occupation in the lower levels of the house, including his kitchen and vestiges of the thirteenth-century hunting lodge, over which his house was built. The fine collection of furniture, rare books, porcelain and other treasures includes paintings by Van Dyck, Kneller, Reynolds and Gainsborough, and also Robert Peake the Elder's famous picture of Queen Elizabeth being borne along on a sedan chair by her nobles, Raleigh among them.

He was the first to introduce tobacco to the English court, and on display is a pipe reputed to have been presented to him by an Indian chief, although how this happened is not clear since Raleigh never set foot in North America. The pipe's authenticity may be questionable, but tests have shown it to be of Virginian maple. At any rate, he is reported to have smoked it on the scaffold before handing it to a relative, the Anglican Bishop Lancelot Andrewes, and it survived a German bomb on London in 1941 which destroyed some accompanying artefacts. In the grounds of Sherborne Castle is the stone seat on which Raleigh is supposed to have sat enjoying a quiet smoke when a servant threw a flagon of ale over him, thinking his master was on fire. Legends have swarmed to the charismatic Raleigh like bees to a honey pot, and this one may be no less true than the unhorsing at Sherborne or the famous laying of his fashionable cloak over mud at Greenwich on the River Thames to protect the queenly slippers.

His Virginia colony had an eventful early career. The James River pioneers suffered desperately from illness, starvation, primitive housing and dissension for three years and were about to abandon the settlement when new settlers and supplies arrived. The colony took permanent root in 1614, four years before Raleigh's execution, when lucrative tobacco exporting began. Five years later the first African slaves arrived and a representative assembly was voted in. These three themes – the tobacco economy, slavery and the struggle for democratic government – were to reverberate through revolution and civil war. Raleigh's contribution to the birth of the United States was honoured in 1882 by a group of Americans who installed a memorial window in St Margaret's Church, Westminster, where he rests with his son Carew and his embalmed head which his faithful widow had saved in a red leather bag.

The modern state of Virginia remembers Raleigh in many proud ways, and North Carolina honours him with the name of its capital, but there is no memorial to him in Sherborne or among the many tributes to lesser notables in the abbey where he and his lady had worshipped. There were recent hopes that the great man's statue standing outside the Ministry of Defence in London would be removed to his Dorset castle, but the decision was made to resite it at Greenwich Naval College instead.

However, Raleigh still haunts his 'fortune's fold'. According to local legend on every 29 October, the day of his execution, his spirit rises among the gaunt ruins of the old castle and wanders through his estate before fading into the woods, but not into obscurity - history sees to that.

2

The Hero of Jamestown

Dorset Admiral Sir George Somers was in command of nine ships carrying desperately needed supplies to Raleigh's troubled colony in Virginia when a violent storm scattered the fleet in the mid-Atlantic. His flagship *Sea Venture* was attended by a two-masted pinnace which began tossing helplessly as mountainous waves swamped the deck. Somers' crew managed to attach a lifeline, but the stricken vessel had to be cut free, and all on board were never seen again. *Sea Venture* was herself in trouble, taking in water and at risk of sinking unless the desperate efforts of the men manning the pumps could keep her afloat long enough to reach dry land, but the North American coast was hundreds of miles and many sailing days away. Then Somers recalled a nearer group of islands he had noted while returning from one of his buccaneering forays in the Caribbean, and a new course was set. Kept afloat by the energetic pumping, his ship reached the largest of the islands and grounded on a coral reef. Crew and passengers scrambled ashore and gave thanks to God for their deliverance. But their relief must have been shaded with anxiety at the sight of their last link with the outside world lying hopelessly wedged offshore, never to sail again. They were castaways on an uninhabited island in a vast ocean.

Somers was typical of the dashing Elizabethan rovers asserting England's growing power on the seas, although his family background was more modest than Raleigh's. He was born on 24 April 1554 under the thatched roof of a family shop in Lyme Regis and might have followed his parents serving behind the counter had he not, at the age of 11 or 12, been tempted by a life at sea like other local lads. The harbour was busy with fishing boats and ships trading with the continent. Little is known about young Somers' early seafaring career, but at some time he was drawn into the privateering expeditions preying on Spanish galleons and bringing their loot back to England, and by the day of his marriage, at the age of twenty-eight, he was fairly well off. His bride was nineteen year old Joane [sic] Heywood, the daughter of a local farmer and landowner and possessed her own property in Lyme Regis. Over the next nine years their combined resources acquired land just outside the town around the thirteenth-century village of Whitchurch Canonicorum, as well as a lease of Berne, a large manorial estate with a mansion which the couple turned into a luxurious home. They were not blessed with children of their own but took over the two young sons of his elder brother Nicholas and his wife, who had died within a few months of each other.

For a while Somers enjoyed domestic bliss and the comfort of a country squire, but he could not deny the call of the sea, and in 1595 he embarked on a series of privateering adventures with licence from Queen Elizabeth. He captained one of a fleet of ships that seized a number of Spanish vessels as prizes off the Iberian coast, the Portuguese Azores, and the Caribbean islands. After sacking a couple of Spanish settlements on the east coast of South America, he called at Cuba on his way home and there met Raleigh, who was also returning to England after capturing valuable prizes but had failed to find the prize closest to his heart, the legendary golden city of El Dorado in Guyana (see Chapter 1 – In Quest of El Dorado). Somers had been invited to join Raleigh's expedition but he had other plans at the time. After the Cuba meeting he took a separate route home and came across the mysterious islands that would dictate his career nearly a decade later.

Over the next three years Somers joined two profitable buccaneering expeditions to the Azores and took a decisive role in the naval action that foiled a Spanish attempt to land an army of 5,000 troops on the coast of Southern Ireland. By now his exploits were gaining recognition in London, and he was rewarded with a knighthood in 1603. He entered Parliament representing Lyme Regis and added his voice to the parliamentary debates on colonisation that culminated in the formation of the Virginia Company, with a revised charter which Elizabeth's successor, James I, readily granted on 23 May 1609, on the promise of a fifth of all the mined ores recovered by the company, notably gold, of course. Somers became a shareholder and an executive officer, and when the Jamestown colony began to falter, he was appointed admiral of the ships that left Plymouth on 2 June 1609 with relief supplies and more colonists. He was never to see England again.

By the heroic efforts of his crew, the *Sea Venture* survived the Atlantic storm that dispersed the fleet and limped to safety in the chain of uninhabited islands vast distances from anywhere. They proved to be extremely fertile with an agreeable climate and a plentiful supply of food from the tropical fruit, fish, wild hog, and birds and eggs. The urge to settle down in this earthly paradise was strong among the 150 men and women who had joined the *Sea Venture* with the expectation of a new life in Virginia, but Somers was determined to resume their mercy mission to Jamestown. He ordered his men to build two pinnaces with timber hacked from the island's abundant cedar trees and salvage from the hapless *Sea Venture*. After months of strenuous work, *Patience* and *Deliverance* were ready for the voyage to Jamestown. The passengers had, however, given up their ambition to join the settlers in Virginia and preferred to remain where they were rather than risk their lives again in unproven vessels.

Laden with salted fish and hog-meat for the settlers suffering in Jamestown, the two pinnaces survived a month on the ocean and sailed into Chesapeake Bay to a joyful reception from the hungry colonists. Somers and his crew had been given up for lost, but a shock awaited them; the Virginian settlers had endured sickness and privation and decided to return to England on the ships that had survived the disastrous storm of two years before. The fleet headed for the open Atlantic with Somers once more at the helm. By coincidence, they met three relief ships bringing more provisions and migrants from England, and Somers gave the order to his captains to go about and return to Jamestown. Now there was food for empty bellies, but there were more mouths to feed. To stave off a seemingly inevitable disaster, the admiral offered to sail *Patience* back to the island for provisions, an offer that was warmly applauded. A larger vessel that joined as escort went back to Jamestown after a storm separated the pair. Despite the pounding wind and waves, Somers forged on alone to the island, took on supplies of food, and returned to Jamestown. He repeated the exercise and was hailed as the saviour of the Virginian colony. By accident, he was the founder of another British colony - Bermuda.

The violent storm, the shipwreck, the heroic ferrying of life-saving supplies to Jamestown - all these stresses took their toll on his health, and while on the island preparing for yet another attempt to take succour to the Jamestown settlers, he fell terminally ill, supposedly from food poisoning. He died on 9 November 1610 at the age of fifty-six.

Author David Raines relates in *Sir George Somers, a Man and His Times*, published in 1984, that there was some confusion over what happened next. Apparently, a nephew who had taken part in the Virginian episode, Matthew Somers, wanted to carry out his uncle's instructions and take his body back for burial in Dorset, but there was a difference of opinion on board *Patience*.

Eventually, it was decided to leave the admiral's heart on the island, and Matthew sailed the pinnace to Lyme Regis with his uncle's body in June 1611. The town was overjoyed at the return of their loved ones; the only news of their fate had been brought by a ship that had returned from Jamestown and reported the disappearance of *Sea Venture* in the storm, but their relief was tempered by the sight of the admiral's coffin. On 4 June he was laid to rest in the ancient church in Whitchurch Canonicorum, where a brass plate in his memory was unveiled 297 years later – on 25 July 1908. A stone shrine in the church contains bones believed to be those of its patron saint, St Wite, and there are three oval holes through which disabled pilgrims would place their affected limbs in the expectation of a cure.

Somers is sometimes called the discoverer of Bermuda, and the charter granted by James I recognised the new colony as Somers Isles, and the group was known as such until records were recovered showing that it had been seen by mariners as early as 1511. Four years later the islands were mapped by Juan de Bermudez, and it is the Spanish navigator's name by which they are known today. However, they lacked people until Somers landed, and the colony celebrates him as its founder. Where his flagship grounded is preserved in their history as Sea Venture Reef, but exactly where his heart was buried is not certain, although a plaque in Somers' Gardens in the capital, St George's, suggests it was there. His adventure is said to have inspired Shakespeare to write *The Tempest*, sometimes regarded as the Bard's finest play, in which Prospero's island appears as the Bermoothes. Bermuda has remained loyal to the Crown, although unofficially it traded with the Americans in

Artefacts found on the wreck of the *Sea Venture* in Bermuda. (Bermuda Maritime Museum)

the rebellion for Independence and again in the Civil War. Since the early 1800s it has served as a strategic base for the British and US navies, and is currently popular with American and Canadian visitors as a holiday resort.

A proud little town

The smallest of Dorset's three ports, Lyme Regis, clings to a beautiful stretch of coast looking as if it had slipped down a cleft in the nearby hills and would have plunged into the sea but for the restraint of the harbour edge. The steep through-road tests walkers and low gears in either direction as it climbs back towards the hills. For all its smallness, Lyme can boast a long and eventful career. It was recorded in history as long ago as 1096 as a small fishing village and grew in stature because of its access to the sea. In 1284 Edward I granted the Royal Charter which added Regis to its name and gave the inhabitants a greater say in their own affairs, and in the same century the curving arm embracing the harbour, known locally as the Cobb, was constructed to protect the anchored shipping from the moods of the English Channel.

Thirty-four years after Somers' death, his hometown was plunged into the violence of the Civil War that erupted when the nation's Protestant Parliament rose against the despotic Charles II. A besieging army commanded by his son, Prince Maurice, battered the town with cannons and fire-arrows, but the townsmen fought back with muskets loaded by their womenfolk dressed as men to give the impression the defenders were stronger in numbers than they were, and after two months Maurice led his frustrated force away as the Earl of Essex approached with parliamentary troops.

Lyme Regis was again in turmoil when in June 1688 three ships sailed into the harbour with eighty armed men commanded by the Duke of Monmouth, the eldest of the twelve illegitimate children of Charles II, whose marriage to Catharine of Braganza was barren. A Protestant, the Duke was launching a foolish and ill-starred attempt to foment a national rebellion and wrench the throne from James II, the late king's brother who was a Catholic.

The Duke chose this part of England for its strong Protestant sentiment, and over the next three weeks he recruited a third of the male residents of Lyme Regis to join him on a march north through Dorset and neighbouring counties, gathering a raggle-taggle army of supporters along the way. Armed mainly with pitchforks and farming implements, they never numbered more than 8,000, and inevitably were trounced at the Battle of Sedgmoor by the king's soldiers, who treated the survivors savagely. Monmouth fled back to Dorset, but was discovered hiding in a ditch at Holton in the north of the county, and he and his companions were tried and executed. Among the rebels sent to the gallows by the infamous Judge Jeffrys were thirteen Lyme men who were buried in the parish churchyard.

The Pitchfork Rebellion had been backed by the King of Holland, William of Orange, who landed further along the coast in 1688 with an army and his wife

Mary, the Protestant daughter of James II, and succeeded where Monmouth had failed; he reigned over Britain for fifty years.

The town is now a magnet for visitors and a haven for pleasure boats. Its picturesque charms have been tenaciously preserved over the centuries and drawn a number of celebrated writers, among them Jane Austen, who wrote her last novel *Persuasion* during her stay and is remembered by a public open space, the Jane Austen Garden. Best known among the modern scribes is the late John Fowles, whose novel *The French Lieutenant's Woman* was made into the film with that memorable scene where the lonely figure of Meryl Streep stands on the Cobb gazing forlornly out to sea, as many a Lyme Regis widow must have done.

3

A Pilgrims' Father

The founder of Virginia and the British Empire was languishing in the Tower of London under sentence of death in the year 1606 when, a few hilly miles from Sir Walter Raleigh's home at Sherborne Castle, a reformist parson fresh from Oxford arrived in Dorset to become the new rector of the county town, Dorchester. The Reverend John White devoted the next fourteen years of his life to transforming the wayward county town into a model of Puritan living, and then came the world-shaping event in 1620 that was to stretch his vision beyond the bounds of his ancient parish - the landing of the Pilgrim Fathers on the New England coast. Those anxious fugitives from the religious oppression of Stuart England had scanned the shore from the storm-battered deck of the *Mayflower* before scrambling on to the sandy peninsular immortalised in world history as Cape Cod, which curls into the Atlantic like a symbolic finger beckoning others to follow. John White responded by gathering moral and financial support to offer the same prospect of religious freedom to the folk of Dorset and adjoining counties, and in 1625 an advance party sailed from Weymouth, eight miles from his parish. They were the first of the Dorchester Pilgrims, as they are revered in American history, who were destined to play a founding role in the settlement of another British colony, Massachusetts.

Besides his spiritual motive, White had a practical purpose; he wanted to help the fishermen of Weymouth and the other Dorset ports of Poole and Lyme Regis, who each year were braving 3,000 treacherous miles of ocean to harvest the teeming cod off the coasts of New England and Newfoundland. He believed his settlers and the crops they raised could provide the sailors with a sheltering land base and fresh food. It was also in his evangelical mind that there would be native American souls to harvest in the name of Christianity.

By a quirk of history, the city of Dorchester had itself been a colonial settlement. To the Romans it was known as Durnovaria, after the British tribe they subdued around AD 70, and the conquerors left behind a rich legacy of archaeological remains and a typical grid-pattern of city streets. Their natural amphitheatre with terraces cut into the chalk continued to entertain the townsfolk through and beyond medieval times, and as recently as 1705 the spectators watched the judicial strangling and burning on a pyre of a young woman convicted of poisoning her unfaithful husband.

When the new rector took his first steps into the pulpit of St Peter's, the largest of his three churches, his immediate concerns were his pending marriage later in the year and, above all, the challenge of realising in Dorchester his Puritan conviction that a community could and should be ruled by the lessons of the Bible. As a Fellow of Oxford he had listened to the other scholars arguing for the doctrinal 'purification' (the word that gave rise to the Puritan label) of the established church and the elimination of what they regarded as 'Popish' influences. They felt encouraged when Elizabeth I, a Catholic although head of her father's breakaway English church, was succeeded after her death by James I, who had been trained in the Presbyterian mould in his native Scotland where he reigned as James VI. However, for personal reasons he did not love the creed that would abolish the mitred bishops upon whom he relied to uphold the royal presumption of a divine right to rule, and he vowed to 'harry' (harass) Nonconformists and force them from his kingdom.

The new monarch's claim to be above papal authority so incensed a group of Catholic extremists that they plotted in 1605 to ignite a rebellion throughout the land by blowing up Parliament at the opening of a new session – and His Majesty with it.

Gunpowder secreted in the cellars under the chamber was ready to open up the proceedings without ceremony, but on the previous night the thirty-six deadly barrels were discovered, along with a terrorist named Guy Fawkes. Since then his effigy is burnt on bonfires across the land on every 5 November, although not everyone knows or cares why, for it is an excellent excuse for disposing of autumnal rubbish and frightening old ladies and domestic pets with noisy fireworks. Guy Fawkes and his fellow conspirators were executed for their treachery, among them Sir Everard Digby, a relative of the Earl of Bristol, John Digby, who bought the Sherborne manor that the Crown sequestrated after Raleigh's downfall for alleged treason. Explosives and weapons were said to have been found in his castle.

A few days after the foiling of the Gunpowder Plot, the unscathed sovereign awarded the Dorchester vacancy to White, who made no secret of his leaning towards Presbyterianism but had no 'explosive', that is to say, immoderate designs, on the way the state church was run. He preferred to seek reforms by persuasion and example, and unlike the despairing dissidents, he believed that the church could be reformed from within. He probably owed his moderation to a conventional upbringing by parents whose joint ancestry had followed a long tradition of loyalty to the establishment. His father (another Reverend John White) and mother Isabel could boast a former bishop of Winchester in Hampshire, a Lord Mayor of London, and a mayor of fifteenth-century Calais, when the French port was an English possession. Over Christmas 1575 they welcomed the birth of the future rector of Dorchester, the second son of their seven children. The family was living at that time in the village of Stanton St John, five miles from Oxford, where White senior held a university post. Later he moved south to Salisbury as chancellor of the cathedral and is buried there. John junior studied at Winchester College and then at Oxford where he emulated his father and became Warden of New College.

Dorchester had been without a senior cleric for seven years when White took over the living, his first since leaving college, and the social and moral climate was in decline. He threw his vigour and commitment into the task of transforming the town into a community where people were soberly dressed, despised sloth and leisure as sins, prized formal education, and looked after the poor and needy. He is described by one historian as being 'severe but not austere', and unlike the more committed Puritans, he was not averse to his flock enjoying themselves, provided the fun was what he regarded as morally correct. Not everyone agreed with his sermons, but the general improvement in the community's life and government was undeniable.

Ironically, White's holy campaign was stalled by a devilish disaster. The Great Fire of Dorchester in August 1613 destroyed half of the flourishing city in one day. Not unusually for those times, it began in a candle-maker's shop and spread rapidly, consuming merchants' buildings and the thatched and largely wooden homes of shopkeepers and working people. Men and women rushed from the fields to fight the blaze, and prisoners were let out of jail to help fetch water from the River Frome. Five of the prisoners were afterwards rewarded with pardons for their efforts. As the flames licked closer to the county headquarters at Shire Hall, there were fears for the gunpowder stored inside. Forty-five barrels were hastily wrapped in wet sheets and rolled to safety, an act that saved the town from being blown apart, but by dusk 170 homes and other buildings lay smouldering in ashes. White's three churches were damaged; St Peter's in the town centre, Holy Trinity at the west end, and, worst hit of all, All Saints at the other end of town where the humblest dwellings had been closer together. The faithful regarded the calamity as a heaven-sent warning to erring leaders of the town and to the robbers, drunks, rowdies, wife-beaters and adulterers to mend their ways.

A Free School and a workhouse-cum-hospital were opened, relief for the homeless, sick and elderly was stepped up, and charity donations increased. The churches became so active and crowded they had to be enlarged. Acknowledging White's practical leadership, the citizens accepted the reforms despite a painful doubling in the parish impost.

The town's Free School was rebuilt after a second fire destroyed thirty properties in 1622, and it was there that White called a meeting of supportive landowners, businessmen and churchmen to finance his dream of an American Dorchester. Adopting the example of the original Pilgrim Fathers, they formed a joint-stock enterprise, the Dorchester Company, and the 121 investors raised £3,000 (White chipped in with £50) to fund the new settlement. They hoped to recoup the outlay by engaging in the long-established custom of West Country fishermen, who each spring dared the Atlantic for the teeming cod banks off Newfoundland. Traditionally, the seamen landed their catches on the American shore to be dried and salted by spare crews they left behind. Up to thirty boats from the Dorset ports were engaged in the trade, which was intended mainly for European markets. White worried about the crews exiled from their families for up to nine months at a time without proper accommodation, fresh food or spiritual guidance (with which he was particularly concerned), and believed that their hardship could be relieved by the permanent farming/fishing settlement he planned. The company secured a patent to settle the land through the good offices of a stockholder, Richard Bushrod, Dorchester's Member of Parliament and a rich merchant who traded in fish and furs brought from America.

The new sails of the *Fellowship* were hoist for its maiden voyage to Massachusetts in March 1625. White and his followers prayed for a successful venture in God's name, but unfortunately it had started late, and on the ship's return with prepared cod the intended market in Spain was already satiated, so that only £200 was raised against the cost of £800. The *Fellowship* tried again in the autumn, followed by the 40 ton *Amytie,* but these trips and others were unprofitable on the whole, and in its third year the Dorchester Company collapsed.

White's dream of a new Dorchester in America was being realised, nevertheless. There were now forty-six settlers at the place they knew as Cape Anne, the present day Gloucester in Massachusetts. To make the most of the fine natural harbour, they had built a landing-stage to cater for the waterborne trade, but most of them were not fisher folk and after two and a half years, some decided to move from their bleak location to the Indian district of Naumkeig, about a dozen miles inland where there was rich grassland for the cattle shipped from England. Their community, Salem (meaning peaceful), became anything but peaceful. To their founder's dismay the very intolerance from which his Dorchester Pilgrims had escaped in England was beginning to grip Salem. All faiths except Puritanism were barred, and the bigotry led to the notorious witchcraft trials of 1692 and the hanging of nineteen men and women.

White kept in touch with the Dorchester Pilgrims and was active in the formation of the Massachusetts Bay Company, which absorbed the Dorchester Company's interests in 1629 and won a charter from the newly-crowned Charles I. The new company recognised the lesson of Roanoke that successful colonisation required better organisation and resources than small ventures could offer. Most of the shareholders were Puritans, but as rich London businessmen they mixed their spiritual and commercial motives in a combination that was to cause White some misgivings, and he felt obliged to remind them of the high-minded purpose of the original pioneers.

Under Charles, the High Church antagonism towards non-conforming Anglicans intensified, and the trickle of dissentients to New England was about to become a flood. The following summer nearly 1,000 men and women crowded into a fleet of seventeen ships, the largest English emigration yet. Before the *Mary and John* left Plymouth with 140 men and women emigrants from Dorset and the south-west, White travelled from Dorchester to preach the farewell sermon.

Some months earlier he had gone to the Tower of London and tried unsuccessfully to speak to his friend and supporter Denzil Holles, parliamentary representative for Dorchester, who had been locked up along with four other members after causing a furore in the assembly. They had forcefully held the protesting Speaker in his chair to allow the passing of resolutions condemning the king's attempts to raise taxes without parliamentary consent and to introduce innovations into church practices which were regarded by Nonconformists as incipient 'popery', in view of Charles' recent marriage to a Catholic queen. The king, having failed to have his way with a rebellious Parliament, dissolved it. During the eleven despotic years that followed, Charles grew more desperate for funds as a result of his disastrous wars with France and Spain and armed attacks on the Scots, and the inevitable reaction came in 1642; England plunged into civil war.

Dorset landowner Sir Walter Erle, a prominent supporter of the Dorchester Pilgrims and squire of the 800 acre Charborough Park, led a body of rebels to secure the county coastal region for Parliament, including the naval base at Portland, and thought he had succeeded. Dorchester declared unflagging allegiance to his cause, threw up defences, ordered gun carriages from a carpenter, and trained a militia to besiege Raleigh's castle in Sherborne which had remained staunchly Royalist. But on the approach of the enemy Dorchester surrendered without a fight. A nephew of the king, Prince Maurice, trotted his horse to County Hall at the head of the cavalry and took command of the Royalist force, but in spite of his assurance that the residents had nothing to fear, his ill-disciplined soldiery took to robbing properties, and the book-lined study in the rectory was pillaged. Distraught, White fled to London with fellow priest William Benn and saw out the war as rector of the London suburb of Lambeth.

Dorchester warmly welcomed the victorious Roundheads in 1645, and White returned to his rectory, but things were not the same. Besides criticism of the priestly absence in the city's time of trial, there was increasing talk of disaffected congregations breaking away from the state church. Separatism was never part of White's philosophy, and as a member of the Parliament-approved Westminster Assembly of Divines, he was helping formulate a system that would integrate Presbyterianism into the Anglican establishment. To 'prevent heresies', as he called the splinter tendency, in March 1647 he held a special fast in St Peter's. There was poverty in the town, too, worsened by the hostilities at home and abroad that had decimated the English wool trade, Dorchester's principal source of income, and the parish was unable to pay his stipend. In financial difficulty, and old and feeble after forty-three years as rector and now a widower, he died on 21 July 1648. The funeral service was simple, as he would have wished, and the mourners showed their true appreciation of his work by draping the porch of St Peter's in black for more than a month.

He had been troubled by developments affecting his Dorchester Pilgrims. Those who sailed in the *Mary and John* had been led by a Massachusetts Bay stockholder, Roger Ludlow, who bought the vessel before it sailed and on arrival in New England selected twelve of the men for a 100-mile trek through the wilderness. At Matapan they established a township in what is now Connecticut.

They suffered greatly from privation but were gradually joined by more pioneers from Dorset and the West Country, and the new Dorchester prospered, in spite of Indian wars in which many of the immigrants died and hundreds of Indian warriors and families were slaughtered by their Christian saviours. Squaws and their children were torched in their wigwams. Several of the expeditions against the Indians were headed by a Devon man, John Endicott, who had sailed from Weymouth in 1628 aboard the Dorchester Company's ship *Abigail* to become the deputy governor and eventually governor of Massachusetts. He is credited with founding the first Puritan church in Salem and gained the reputation of a narrow-minded bigot who banned merriment or deviation of any kind. When two of the brethren tried to read services from the Anglican book of prayer, he had them sent back to England; other suspected deviants were flogged. He died in Boston, one of the townships springing up along the coast. Notwithstanding his reputation, in 1914 a memorial to him was unveiled in Weymouth by a descendant, Mrs Josephine Chamberlain.

The American Dorchester changed to Windsor in 1637, but its name survives as a district of Boston. The early pioneers had regarded themselves as planters, not colonials, and clung to their English roots but, as Irish and other nationalities poured in, the colony developed independently of the home country and called itself the Commonwealth of Massachusetts, regardless of what the king thought. Massachusetts, named after an Indian chief, was later a leading colony in the independence struggle, and its representational method of government was the model chosen for the constitution of the United States. David Underwood relates in *Fire from Heaven*, his exhaustive study of seventeenth-century life in the English Dorchester, that the early pioneers played 'an important part' in establishing the infant colonies of Massachusetts and Connecticut. Frances Rose-Troup goes further in her definitive biography *John White* and calls him 'Founder of Massachusetts'.

Little is known about the rector's married life. It can be imagined that his wife Anne, née Burges, was a devoted Presbyterian since the reformist strain ran through her family. Her brother, the Reverend John Burges, was frequently at odds with the orthodox church in Cambridgeshire for preaching against the ceremonies and refusing to wear the surplice, and was imprisoned for his fiery views. Anne bore four sons, one of whom followed his father into the church, two went into commerce in Dorchester, and the youngest is said to have fought in the parliamentary forces as a captain during the Civil War. Anne is thought to have died in the same year as her husband, 1648. Some of White's relatives settled in Dorset, including his sister Mary who moved to Dorchester after losing her husband, a rector in the neighbouring county of Wiltshire.

John White, generally regarded as 'the Patriarch of Dorchester', was laid to rest at St Peter's Church where a memorial brass plate in the porch records, 'A man of great godliness, good scholarship and wonderful ability and kindness, he had a very strong sway in this town. He greatly set forward the emigration to the Massachusetts Bay colony where his name lives in unfading remembrance.' He had regarded vanity as a sin during his lifetime, and such a well-merited commendation to his God might have embarrassed the modest father of the Dorchester Pilgrims. Who knows?

The Dorchester Heritage Committee has erected a memorial that appropriately sums up White's eventful career in the following words:

Fellow of New College, Oxford, 1600-1606, he organised the National Relief Campaign after the Great Fire of Dorchester in 1613; from 1620 he organised the funds and procured the charters for three companies which established the colony of Massachusetts. The settlers sailed in 1624-26 on 'Fellowship', 'Amytie', and 'Pilgrime'; in 1627 on 'Peeter', 'Happy Entrance', and 'Abigail'; and in 1629 on 'Arabella', 'Lyons Whelp' and 'Mary and John'. From 1640-46 he also resided in London where he was a leading member and chairman of the Assembly of Divines. His house was plundered and his library stolen by a party of Prince Rupert's Horse. From 1643 he was rector of St Mary's, Lambeth, where the Devil is said to have appeared in his bedroom. After a long wait White remarked, 'If thou hast nothing else to do, I have', turned away and went to sleep.

4

Seizing the Maine Chance

A year before the first of John White's pilgrims sought religious freedom in Massachusetts, soldier-sailor Robert Gorges left his home at Bradpole in West Dorset and sailed from Weymouth with a very different motive in mind, one more in keeping with the Raleigh ambition of acquiring wealth. He landed a party of settlers on the rocky shore to the north of Massachusetts, named the settlement Weymouth after their port of departure, and claimed the land on behalf of his father, Sir Ferdinando Gorges, who is respected today as the founder of Maine, the most north-easterly state of the US.

Sir Ferdinando, a descendant of a Norman family of Dorset landowners, the de Gorges, was one of the English entrepreneurs whose eyes had been opened to the money-making potential of the New World by the growing commercial success of Raleigh's tobacco colony in Virginia, and a number of European adventurers, among them French as well as British, tried to establish permanent footholds in Maine. Recent archaeological evidence suggests that the Vikings had preceded them as early as the eleventh century, but none of the settlements survived the harsh winters and Indian raids. An Italian navigator sponsored by the English crown went ashore there in 1597 and looked in vain for treasure. American Indians were occasionally brought to an England fascinated by their native dress, and when five arrived at Plymouth in 1605, Sir Ferdinando, the military governor of the West Country port, took charge of three of them. They learned enough English to describe their homeland in such seductive detail that the distinguished soldier, knighted for his services to the French King Henry IV in the Wars of Religion in France, began to think seriously of colonising Maine. He obtained a charter from James I and organised a company of merchant adventurers who funded several fishing and trading expeditions to the territory, but only one over-wintered.

At the age of fifty-seven the enterprising soldier might have thought himself too old to embark on colonial adventures, but for whatever reason he intended to pass the Royal patent on to the elder of his two sons, and it was Robert Gorges who in the autumn of 1623 followed in the wakes of the many Weymouth vessels then engaged in a lucrative trade with North America. After ensuring that his pioneer gentlemen, servants and others were well settled into their new land, Robert handed the governorship over to a Scottish scholar, David Thomson, who had been in New England since the spring. Robert returned to England in the following year, 1625, the year that the Dorchester Pilgrims sailed the other way.

Some months later Britain's infant colonies acquired a new sovereign. The Gorges territory acquired the name of an old French province, Maine, which belonged to the new queen, Henrietta Maria, daughter of Henry IV of France. By historical coincidence, her proprietary had twice been an English possession in the twelfth and fifteenth centuries.

Robert died soon after his return from Maine. Prolonged litigation challenged his father's ownership of the whole of the province and did not end in his favour until the grant of a new charter in 1639. Throughout the seventeenth century and into the next, the Catholic French ensconced in New Brunswick disputed the northern boundary of Maine as the two nations struggled for control of North America. To protect itself against French intervention, Protestant Massachusetts annexed Maine during the Commonwealth period of Republican rule in Britain, and then in 1763 France conceded its sovereignty over Canada and adjoining territories under the Treaty of Paris. Peace came to Maine – but not for long.

The thirteen colonies led by Massachusetts rose against British 'taxation without representation', as they put it, and fought for independence. The opposing armies marched to and fro across Maine until the American victory, and then came the Civil War in which Maine fought on the Union side. The province's anti-slavery stance was personified by one of its best known residents, Harriet Beecher Stowe, the author of *Uncle Tom's Cabin*. Even after hostilities ceased between the republic and loyalist Canada, the delineation of the boundary between Maine and New Brunswick was not agreed until 1842, by which time Maine had been severed from Massachusetts and admitted as the twenty-third state of the Union.

The role of the Gorges family in the founding of Maine is history, but Dorset's contribution is alive and well. The state's chief commercial city and onetime capital shares its name with the naval base commanding the entrance to Weymouth harbour, from which Robert Gorge and his pioneers caught their last glimpse of Dorset as they sailed to forge the county's link with Maine.

5

Lord in a Manor of Speaking

Virginia and Massachusetts were already going concerns when an Englishman with an Irish title and property interests at Christchurch on the Dorset[1] coast sent two shiploads of settlers across the Atlantic and added Maryland to the burgeoning British empire in North America. The second Lord Baltimore was realising the colonising ambitions of his late father, who had died before his plans for a southern colony could be achieved.

The first of the Baltimore line was a cultured Yorkshireman who studied at Oxford, entered parliament as plain George Calvert, and rose to become Secretary of State and Sir George in the government of James I. The king was keen to expand the English and Scottish presence in Ireland and granted him 2,300 acres of that troublesome island. Calvert also acquired a new faith from his Irish connection. Conversion to Catholicism ended his political career, because he now had to recognise the Pope and not the Protestant king as the supreme head of the breakaway English church, and he dutifully resigned from His Majesty's government. Although James was foresworn to defend and maintain the Protestant faith in his kingdom, he nevertheless prized Calvert's unswerving loyalty and gave him membership of the Privy Council, the advisory body to the Crown, and a seat in the House of Lords. Calvert took his title, Baltimore, from the name of his Irish estate and served as a Privy Councillor until James died in 1625, when Calvert's recusancy precluded him from taking the obligatory oath of allegiance to Charles I, who succeeded his father to the throne.

Calvert was rich now. Feeling the contemporary urge for investment in colonies, he bought an interest in the London & Bristol Company for the Plantation of Newfoundland with an eye to founding settlements on the island and a lucrative two-way trade with England. At that time Dorset fishermen were competing with others from the West Country and the European mainland for the teeming cod in the coastal waters. The English hauls were not only helping to feed the folk at home and the men in the Royal Navy but fuelling the nation's growing economic and political power with exports.

---

1 Christchurch, formerly in Hampshire, transferred to neighbouring Dorset in 1974.

Calvert established his first settlement at Placentia Bay in the south-east of Newfoundland. James I was on the throne, and two years later, in 1623, he granted Calvert a charter for the whole of the adjoining peninsular on a token payment of two Indian arrows to be delivered annually to Windsor Castle. Calvert aimed £25,000 at his colonial target, building granaries, stores, and the largest dwelling on the island which he occupied in 1628 with his wife and family. The intense international competition for the offshore treasure obliged him to fund two ships to end harassment by French vessels, six of which were captured, and he complained to the Duke of Buckingham, a confidant of the king. 'I came to reap and sow,' he wrote, 'but I am fain to fighting with Frenchmen who have disquieted me and many other of His Majesty's subjects fishing in this land.'

There was another cause for Calvert's discontent; he had drawn on his classical learning for the name of his settlement, Avalon, after the paradise of Celtic legend, but a year in Newfoundland persuaded him its climate was less than sublime, and he wrote to King Charles:

> I have found by too dear bought experience that from the middlest of October to the middlest of May there is a sadd fare of winter upon all this land.

He went on:

> I am determined therefore to commit this place to fishermen that are able to encounter storms and hard weather, and to remove myself with some forty persons to your Majesty's dominion of Virginia where, if your Majesty will be pleased to grant me a precinct of land with such privileges as the King your father, my gracious master (did), I shall endeavour to the utmost of my power to deserve it.

In other words, he could do with another Royal Charter.

Without waiting for a reply, after only twelve months in Avalon he moved his family south to Virginia, expecting a warm welcome as an investor and board director of the Virginia Company, which owned the thriving colony, but the Catholic newcomer was cold-shouldered by the Protestant community. Undeterred, he complained to the king that the Newfoundland paradise had stricken half his settlers with sickness and taken the lives of ten of them, and he repeated his suggestion that if he were granted the fertile, undeveloped wilderness he had seen on the opposite bank of the Potomac from Virginia, it could become a proud new British colony fit for Catholics. Charles, although nominally a Protestant, happened to be married to a devout Catholic, and he granted Calvert a charter making him proprietor for this latest addition to the British Empire. It was named Maryland in honour of his French-born queen, Princess Henrietta Maria.

Before the Royal seal could be stamped on the charter, however, Calvert died in April 1632 at the age of fifty-three. The grant passed to his twenty-seven year old second son, Caecilius, more generally known as Cecil, who had remained in

England and escaped the watery fate of some of his siblings who were reportedly drowned when the barque returning them to England foundered in a storm. On becoming the second Lord Baltimore, Cecil wasted no time in pursuing his father's wishes, and with financial backing from relatives and supporters he bought and equipped the 750 ton *Ark of Avalon*, only 110ft from stem to stern, and also a pinnace, *Dove,* that was even smaller. On this diminutive flotilla he proposed to launch his would-be Marylanders, most of whom were Protestant farm workers and artisans, but among them were some Catholic sons of the landed gentry backing the enterprise. These privileged young men, with their accompanying servants and two Jesuit priests, would attempt to create a Catholic enclave sandwiched between the Protestant colonies of Virginia and New England.

Before the chosen set sail, they received a message from their sponsor. Remembering the bigotry his father had encountered at home, Baltimore urged them to practise tolerance in their new land and watch out for what he called 'religious plots'. They must make friends of their neighbours in Virginia and plant sufficient crops to feed themselves. They should try to convert the American Indians and not fight them, but at the same time they must prepare defences and train able-bodied men in military skills just in case. The sentiments for harmony were sincere, but the mixed bag of pioneers was taking with it the social and religious divides of the motherland, as the ensuing years would reveal.

On 22 November 1633, the *Ark* and the *Dove* began their perilous voyage, and as they beat along the coast of southern England towards the open sea, Baltimore might well have been able to see them from Christchurch, if he were there and the helmsmen had chosen this alternative way round the Isle of Wight. Wherever he was, his thoughts must have been with the brave souls bearing his colonial ambitions. He had hoped to lead the expedition, but because of the worsening political atmosphere in England following the king's dismissal of the so-called Short Parliament (it lasted only a few weeks) he decided to stand by the beleaguered royal who had ennobled his father. He appointed his younger brothers Leonard and George to look after his interests in Maryland, the former as the first governor. Henceforth, he would rule his distant domain through appointees and never set foot on it.

A few nights out from England the ships were engulfed by a ferocious storm. Tossing wildly, the tiny *Dove* showed a distress lantern and then disappeared in the darkness. The *Ark* had a mainsail ripped in two, but despite the Atlantic weather and the ever-present pirate menace, it managed to struggle the 3,000 miles of ocean to safety in Barbados. The emigrants had paid a terrible price for their delivery; thirty had fallen sick, twelve were dead, and the little pinnace was feared lost. Then, a fortnight later, the *Dove* showed up in the protective company of a British merchantman. The *Ark* must have resounded with cheers of relief and prayers of thanksgiving. United once more, the settlers sailed past North Carolina where Raleigh's unfortunate Roanoke settlement had failed and headed north for Chesapeake Bay and the Potomac. Three months after leaving England the ships anchored in the broad St Mary's River, and in March 1634 the pioneers stepped onto the soil of their promised land. They received a friendly welcome from the Indians, who sold them land on which the settlers built their homes, erected a palisade, and planted crops.

The Maryland charter differed fundamentally from those granted to commercial companies investing in Virginia, Maine and Massachusetts. Baltimore was the sole proprietor, exercising political, judicial and religious autocracy over his 6 million acres of North America. Through his governor, he appointed the administration and the church officials, apportioned the land, commanded security, conferred honours and titles, and issued licences. Enjoying considerable income from the rents and revenues, he ruled his fiefdom like a surrogate prince, answerable only to the sovereign.

While Baltimore's colony was just starting a history, his estate at Christchurch was sharing a venerable one with Raleigh's Sherborne. Both towns stretched back more than 1,000 years to the invading Saxons who brought Christianity from Germany, and then in the eleventh century the Norman conquerors established monasteries and castles to defend their God and their properties. The manors were conveyed in the 1300s to the Montacute (Montague) family for military and political services rendered to Edward III, who also threw in the Salisbury earldom for good measure. However, the Crown repossessed both Christchurch and Sherborne for periods when the Montacutes were out of favour, and the Anglo-French dynasty finally lost them altogether in 1541 when the last of the Plantagenets, the Countess Margaret of Salisbury, was beheaded for having papal sympathies that were anathema to Henry VIII. She was buried at the Tower of London and not in the beautiful tomb she had built for herself and her family in Christchurch Priory. The Tudor king's divorce from the Spanish Princess Catherine of Aragon, had never been accepted by the Vatican, nor had his declaration of himself as the ecclesiastical head in England.

The Merry Monarch demolished the monastic outbuildings erected by the Augustinians at Christchurch Priory, but in a fit of unusual generosity he followed the example set at Sherborne and allowed the townsfolk to have the main building as their parish church - after removing the Priory valuables beforehand. The cathedral-sized edifice was spared and continues its commanding presence over Christchurch and the harbour to this day.

Baltimore acquired Christchurch as a consequence of marriage. He and his wife Anne had been granted the lease of the manor by her father, Lord Arundell, a prominent Catholic peer who bought it in 1601. Upon Arundell's death in 1636 Baltimore assumed the title of Manorial Seigneur of Christchurch on the strength of the lease and, by so-doing, unleashed a bitter family row. Arundell had willed the property to be shared by all his daughters, and there were no less than six of them, Anne being the eldest. All but one of her sisters were married, and the four husbands challenged Baltimore's claim to the revenues and perquisites arising from the estate. They pursued him through the courts for thirty years until common sense finally produced the solution that had been obvious right from the beginning; Christchurch was sold and the proceeds were shared among the litigants. The purchaser and new lord of the manor of Christchurch was the Earl of Clarendon, the most powerful man in England and a member of the group that would run the Carolina colonies (see Chapter 0 - 6 The Earls and the Carolinas). It was no coincidence that Clarendon and the Arundells were well known to each other; the families lived in the same area of Wiltshire. There is a brass memorial to Clarendon's grandfather, Lawrence Hyde, inside the parish church of Tisbury, and many Arundells are buried in the family vault beneath the chancel, thus Maryland's Tisbury stems from the Arundell connection with the Baltimores.

In the background to the long-winded litigation over Christchurch Manor was the worsening political turmoil in England. Charles pitched his kingdom deeper into constitutional crisis as he tried to rule without Parliament, but after eleven years he had to recall the assembly with a desperate plea for funds. His request was thrown out amid disapproval of his expensive hostilities against the Scots, and in frustration he called a general election. Although small in population, Christchurch was entitled by tradition to two Members of Parliament, one representing the dozen burgesses entitled to vote and the other the lord of the manor, and Baltimore determined that both seats should be warmed by Royalists. By now a widower, he wrote from Lincoln's Inn Fields in London on 29 September to:

> My verie [sic] loving freinds the maior and burgesses of Christchurch,

desiring them to vote for his nominee, one Mathew Davys from Shaftsbury in Dorset. The letter went on:

> Thus, not doubting of your freindly [sic] respect to me in this particular according to what you have always done to my predecessors and myself, lords of the manor and burgesses of Christchurch. I bidd you heartily farewell. Your very loving freind. C. Baltimore.

The sly inclusion of himself in his reference to 'lords of the manor' cannot have been lost on the worthies of the town, but if they had any misgivings they generally accepted his claim to the manorial privileges; it was prudent to remember that their 'very loving freind' was their landlord. They adopted Davys after due consideration of his qualifications for office, particularly Baltimore's promise that none of his nominee's expenses would fall on them, and went on to select a local farmer as their second candidate, one Henry Tulse who had represented them in the old Westminster assembly. If Baltimore had hoped to avoid an electoral contest in Christchurch he would have been disappointed; two Parliamentarians leapt into the arena. Henry Wroughton and Lord Lisle were championed by none other than Lord Pembroke who, be it noted, was one of the husbands disputing Baltimore's manorial claim to Christchurch.

Pembroke called on the twelve burgesses to support his candidates, but Mayor John Kemp replied tersely that they had already made their choice, smug in the

Charles Calvert, 3rd Lord Baltimore (1647-1715), Governor of Maryland. (© Philip Mould Ltd, London/The Bridgeman Art Library)

knowledge that they were the only constituents with a vote. As a result of the election Davys and Tulse were sent to Westminster, Wroughton was roundly rejected, and there was no further mention of the rabid anti-Royalist Lisle.

Two years later, in 1642, the new Parliament finally lost patience with the king. In the Civil War Baltimore kept his distance from the conflict, and Christchurch had an easy war. The castle was defended by 200 Royalists, but they and their officers, including a woman captain, surrendered to Cromwell's troops without firing a shot. After peace returned the castle was 'slighted', in Cromwell's words, and reduced to the impotent ruin that is a tourist attraction today. Arundell's fourteenth-century castle at Wardour in Wiltshire did not escape lightly; it was severely damaged by Cromwell's Roundheads and abandoned.

Baltimore's distant colony was proving a headache of a different kind. Within about a year of its founding, the freemen (owners or lessees of land) elected an assembly which began challenging the proprietorial rule. In the first twenty years the growing Protestant population twice took control of Maryland and twice his lordship regained it, but he was obliged in 1638 to concede the right of the majority to pass their own laws, and the assembly adopted an Act of Tolerance which granted freedom of worship to all Christians, regardless of their religious allegiance. This happened in 1649, forty years before William III enacted similar legislation in Britain, with a measure that still excludes Catholics from the throne. The Baltimore proprietary retained its right to veto the assembly's legislation up to the American Revolution.

Looked at overall, Cecil's rule, though aristocratic, was neither despotic nor illiberal. He conceded the institution of an elected assembly, albeit with limited powers, and after his death in 1675 the Baltimore lordship over Maryland continued until the War of Independence ended 140 years of proprietary rule, and the great estates were broken up and redistributed. In neighbouring Pennsylvania, the much-respected Penn dynasty was awarded £130,000 by way of compensation. Only £10,000 went to the final proprietor of Maryland, Henry Harford, who was an illegitimate son of the sixth, last, and least loved of the Baltimore aristocrats.

Maryland still bears reminders of the Baltimore era; the eponymous principal city and Calvert and Cecil counties, for example, and Annapolis which was Anne Arundell Town in honour of Cecil's wife, before being rededicated to Princess Anne of Denmark, the wife of James I, and the state possesses a Tisbury town of its own. London was reminded of the state's founder by a slate and marble memorial which was brought to the British capital by a group of Marylanders in 1996 and mounted on the church wall of St Giles-in-the-Fields, where Cecil is buried, but Christchurch ignores its historic link altogether. There is no plaque, no Maryland Avenue, Baltimore Road, or Calvert Street, and local histories dismiss Baltimore with few words, if they mention him at all. The well-meaning peer who thought he was lord of the manor might never have existed.

To be fair, there are probably few in Maryland or Dorset who know of the transatlantic link of history between them. Did any Marylanders among the US airmen who flew from Christchurch Airfield in the Second World War in support of the Normandy landings realise that the ancient town stretching below the wings of their fighter-bombers had an involvement in the birth of their state? When they left, however, they presented the town with the Union flag that hangs in the twelfth-century parish church – one of the stripes on it is the sole remaining evidence of Maryland in Christchurch.

6

The Earls and the Carolinas

After the restoration of the Stuart dynasty Charles II would have realised from the sketchy maps of North America that there was still some way to go before the British dominated the east coast as his father, Charles I, had wished before his head was removed by the Republican usurpers. Now they too had been removed, and the new wearer of the crown turned to doing something about the empire. In 1663 he sent three ships and 500 soldiers to 'liberate' a Dutch colony separating the British colonies of Maine and Massachusetts in the north from those in the south: Maryland and Virginia. After weak resistance, New Holland re-emerged as New Jersey, and New Amsterdam became New York. There now remained a large territory below Virginia that both England and Spain had claimed but never permanently settled. Charles senior had called it Carolana after a version of his own name, and now his son determined that Carolina, as it is known today, must become a British colony. He gave the organising to eight of his titled cronies, making them the proprietors of land more than twice the size of England and Wales - subject to his overriding rule, of course. Two of the favoured eight would have an historic link with Dorset - Sir Anthony Ashley Cooper, the Lord-Lieutenant of the county and future Earl of Shaftsbury, and the Earl of Clarendon, who would later become the Manorial Lord of Christchurch.

Their distant domain stretched more than 600 miles down the Atlantic coast from Virginia to Spanish-held Florida and inland to the Appalachian Mountains. Spain, France and England had previously attempted footholds, but the sitting residents for the previous 10,000 years, the Amerindians, were still being spared a European takeover more than a century and a half since Columbus and Cabot. The men that Sir Walter Raleigh had settled on Roanoke Island off the Carolina coast in June 1585 lacked the necessary skills and resources to sustain themselves and were having such a hard time when Sir Francis Drake sailed their way in the following summer that he gave most of them a lift home. Had the settlement succeeded, it would have been England's first permanent colony in America.

Among the returnees was a friend of Drake, John White (no relation to the Dorchester rector), who was a gifted artist and had painted exquisite watercolour studies of the Indians and the local flora and fauna which are much prized today. Raleigh appointed him governor of the colony, and he took 107 men, women and children to Roanoke and left them there, including his own family, while he sailed back to England for more supplies. It was 1588, and the Spanish Armada and the invasion scare delayed his return for three years. When he did see the island again he found no trace of the settlers except for their abandoned fort and a few skeletons. The only clue to their disappearance was the word Croatan carved into a tree. This was a reference to the local Indians, and White set off for their village fifty miles away, but his ship sprang leaks in a storm and he changed course for England. Whether the settlers were killed or absorbed into the native culture is a mystery much-debated by historians, but there have been reports of blond-haired, blue-eyed Indians in the area.

British colonialism fared better in Virginia where Raleigh is lauded as the founder, although by the time the first settlement, James Town, was established in 1607, the great Elizabethan had passed his patent to the joint-stock London Company for a share of the profit and was now expecting the loss of his head in the Tower of London.

His jailer, James I, died in 1625 and was succeeded by his son Charles I who granted proprietorship of two further colonies to individuals; Maryland went to Lord Baltimore, and the king's Attorney-General, Sir Robert Heath, became subordinate ruler of Carolina. Heath's domain gathered no settlers, and even after Charles II switched most of the charter to his eight favourites, nothing happened for six or seven years. Then on 15 March 1670, the first permanent residents arrived from England.

Cooper's inclusion among the Carolina proprietors may have been his reward for taking an active role in the negotiations to restore the monarchy after twenty years of Puritan republicanism, although he did show some interest in colonial affairs during an eventful political career. This began in 1640 with his unopposed election to Parliament for Tewkesbury in Gloucestershire, following the example of his father, Sir John Cooper, who had represented the Dorset town of Poole. The ambitious nineteen-year-old law student was technically under-age to stand, but this legal nicety did not matter very much because Charles I, starved for funds, dissolved the uncooperative assembly almost immediately, and the next one was also short-lived. Cooper had been made a ward of court at the age of ten when Sir John died in 1631, leaving his son the family seat at Wimborne St Giles in verdant Dorset, extensive land-ownership across four counties, and considerable debts. The corrupt court commissioners, who included his great-uncle Sir Francis Ashley, put some of the estates up for sale to appease the creditors and bought several themselves at below their market value. Even so, young Cooper remained well-endowed with the Wimborne St Giles estate, profitable plantations in the West Indies, and a quarter-share in a ship trading with the slave coast of West Africa, an early association with the Caribbean and slavery that was to prove significant

When the Civil War erupted in 1642 Sir Ashley Cooper was in his early twenties and rich enough to raise a regiment at his own expense to fight for the embattled king. As colonel he helped secure the surrender of Cromwell's supporters in the Dorset towns of Weymouth and Dorchester, only to be denied the governorship of Weymouth and the neighbouring naval base at Portland that he had been promised. Sir Edward Hyde, the future Earl of Clarendon, was Chancellor of the Exchequer, and he intervened on Cooper's behalf. The king was persuaded to allow the appointment, but, cunningly, only on the expectation that Cooper would resign because of his 'military inexperience'. The compensation of being appointed Sheriff of Dorset and President of the King's Council for the county was apparently not enough. Whether from chagrin or a canny premonition that the Royalists could lose the war, he defected to the enemy, who gave him the command of 1,500 Roundhead soldiers in Dorset. In the autumn of 1644 his men took Wareham and stormed the mansion home of Sir John Strangways at Abbotsbury where the defenders were burned alive. Reportedly, Cooper showed great courage in the action. His force joined other successful actions in Dorset against Sturminster Newton, Shaftsbury and Corfe Castle.

After Cromwell's victory Cooper was little concerned for matters outside his home county for some years until he was returned to Parliament as the member for Poole, his father's old constituency. He had risen in the social scale, having married again a year after the death of his first wife in 1649. His second wife was the sister of the late Earl of Essex, a prominent Presbyterian who had commanded the parliamentary army in the war. Cooper's political stature grew, and as the Puritan regime faltered in 1660 he figured in the negotiations that restored the monarchy. The grateful Charles II appointed him Chancellor of the Exchequer as well as Lord-Lieutenant of Dorset and elevated him to the peerage. Now Baron Ashley, he found himself two years later sharing ownership of Carolina with Clarendon and six other aristocrats.

Clarendon never swerved from loyalty to the Crown. After the toppling of Charles I, he joined the exiled queen and the young Prince Charles in France where he earned the reputation of king-maker during the proceedings that led to the Restoration. Made Lord Chancellor and an earl by Charles II, he took his title from Clarendon Park in Wiltshire, which had historic links with royalty going back at least to 1164 when Henry II's council met there to formulate laws governing the powers of the church over English sovereignty. Although Clarendon was now Britain's most powerful politician, he had originally been intended for the church, but despite his father's wishes he chose the law and was called to the bar at the age of twenty-four. He married for the second time, his first wife having died after six months of wedlock, and was elected to Parliament.

Clarendon might be regarded today as a seventeenth-century spin doctor. As a close adviser and mouthpiece for his cousin, Charles II, he had a seeming influence over the king that aroused suspicion and resentment among his contemporaries, and certainly the close relationship was strengthened by the secret and controversial marriage of his daughter, Anne, to the heir-presumptive, the Duke of York. She became the Queen when the duke ascended the throne as James II. Clarendon's qualifications to be a colonial proprietor were persuasive, for he had helped set up a permanent administration system for the colonies and was a member of the general council for foreign plantations. Perhaps he was obliged to be tolerant, but the stern defender of the king's authority over the established church allowed freedom of worship in the Virginian and Jamaican colonies and extended the same tolerance to Carolina. In England, however, he led the king to expect orthodoxy in religious observance, a stricture that caused the Elders in Christchurch to sack an independently-minded vicar. This was in 1660 and five years before Clarendon bought the little harbour town with an eye to its commercial possibilities as a maritime rival to the thriving port of Portsmouth further along the coast.

Both he and Ashley and their fellow members of the Carolina enterprise – the Duke of Albemarle, the Earl of Craven, Lord John Berkeley, and the knights George Carteret, John Colleton and William Berkeley – regarded their American colony primarily as a source of financial gain. They never paid a visit and are accused of doing little towards its development. Ashley, to give him credit, was concerned enough to commission a proper constitution from his private secretary, John Locke, though he could not have realised at the time that he was being party to a step of awesome historical significance. Locke later became one of England's best-known political philosophers, and his assertion that the governed, and not the governor, should wield the ultimate authority in any civilised country profoundly influenced the world's most powerful democracy, the United States.

After years of apparent inactivity the absentee landlords must have been relieved and delighted to learn that wealthy planters in the British colony of Barbados were looking for land on which to grow rice outside the confines of the Caribbean. So it was that six years after receiving the charter the noble proprietors launched their first settlers in the direction of Carolina. The plan was to call in at Barbados, but one of the three ships sank before it could reach the island and another was wrecked afterwards in a storm off the Bahamas. Two replacements were found, and in May 1670 the little fleet sailed into the only deepwater haven on the coast of Carolina and established Charles Town, the first permanent settlement in the territory. On the way up the coast about a dozen of the settlers had been murdered by Indians during a brief look ashore for drinking water, and of the several hundred men, women and children who had embarked on the horrendous voyage from Plymouth eight months before, only 148 had survived.

The proprietors encouraged the Barbadians to stake out plantations for the growing of rice and later indigo on the coastal flatlands of what would become the states of South Carolina and Georgia. The appointment of an elderly Bermudan, Colonel William Sayle, as the colony's first governor, acknowledged the strong West Indian influence in the early development of the province. The planters brought with them the stratified class system of aristocratic England from which they sprang and introduced large numbers of blacks to work the labour-intensive estates. Slavery and landed privilege were to become major issues in the evolution of the future United States. The north of the colony developed very differently from the south. The first settlers were not rich slave-owners recreating feudal England, but relatively poor Scots and Welsh farmers drifting down from Virginia in search of land of their own, and they were joined by Huguenots fleeing anti-Protestant persecution in France. The rugged mountainous region in the north-west attracted Scottish and Irish Calvinist Presbyterians and German-Swiss Lutherans from Pennsylvania. The resultant mix of national identities and religious beliefs would lead to a vigorously independent and self-reliant populace impatient with outside interference.

The latter half of the seventeenth century was a critical one for both Shaftsbury and Clarendon. The former received his earldom, and after becoming Lord Chancellor in 1672 he responded to a public outcry and persuaded Parliament to ban the barbarous practice of kidnapping children for export to the colonies. But his Presbyterian opposition to proposals that would exclude a Catholic from ascending to the throne in the future got him into deep trouble with Charles II's successor, James II, who had converted to Catholicism. Shaftsbury was dismissed from office and had his privileges as Lord-Lieutenant of Dorset taken away. He spent four years locked up in the Tower, and then on release took his seat in the House of Lords. Clarendon, too, fell from grace in his later years. An orthodox Anglican and a vigorous opponent of Presbyterianism, with its aim of abolishing bishops, he attacked any moves that encroached on the sovereign's divine right to rule. His power over the king eventually led to allegations in Parliament that he was advising his master to dissolve the assembly for good. This was regarded as high treason, and he was brought to the point of impeachment by a cabal that included Shaftsbury, his Carolina colleague. In disgrace, Clarendon escaped to France where he died in 1674. He left his title and ownership of Christchurch to his son, but his bold harbour scheme for the town never really materialised, and only the remnants of a protective pier are still visible at low tide. Shaftsbury lived for a further nine years, and in that time he too faced a charge of treason. He spent a second term in prison as a champion of tolerance towards dissenters and of civil liberties, and ended up in exile in Holland, where he died in 1683.

The new Earls Clarendon and Shaftsbury succeeded their fathers on the Carolina group, which was facing mounting problems in the province. Spaniards based on St Augustine in Florida had become alarmed by the rapid spread of British settlements to the north and slaughtered a Scottish community. Two years into the eighteenth century the Carolinians retaliated with equally violent assaults on Spanish settlements. In 1715 festering Indian resentment against two-timing traders and settlers invading the tribal lands without paying for them erupted into the Yamassee War. Settlements were burnt to the ground and their occupants killed. Desperately the Carolinians appealed for help to prevent the annihilation of the colony. The proprietors responded with money, but nothing else; the British government sent arms and ammunition but no soldiers, and the Carolinians had to rely on raising their own army to fight fearful odds. Fortunately, the Yamassee tribe began to lose its warlike intentions on hearing that the fearsome Cherokee warriors were siding with the Carolinians.

The northern settlers were proving troublesome. Defying attempts to collect fees and taxes, they rejected three of the proprietors' governors, threw a fourth into jail, and so intimidated a fifth that he stayed away. Finally, in 1717 the proprietors caved in and granted the northerners their own candidate who was sympathetic to the popular mood, and by this surrender, North Carolina became, in effect, a separate entity. Pirates were another headache. The province felt powerless to protect its shipping, and it took three warships from Virginia to eliminate the murderous Blackbeard, the most notorious villain of them all.

Back in England an angry Parliament was growing impatient at the unrest and challenged the proprietors to hand over the province if they were unwilling or unable to defend it. Faced with disappointing financial returns from their investment, each of the proprietors, including Shaftsbury and Clarendon, took the £7,500 offered in compensation, except for Earl Granville, the son of one of the original proprietors, Sir George Carteret, who held onto his land in the north-west territory, only to have it confiscated in the War of Independence. South and North Carolina became Crown colonies in 1729 and Georgia three years later. Georgia, named after George II, was the last English colony to be established in North America. The founder was army general, philanthropist and Member of Parliament James Oglethorpe, who obtained a Royal Charter to create a refuge for debtors and paupers from Britain and a barrier against Spanish aggression from Florida.

The peaceful departure of the eightsome proprietary was followed in time by bloody revolution and the even bloodier Civil War, in which the first shot was fired in South Carolina. The three states have preserved their British past and Dorset links; the capital of North Carolina is Raleigh.

7

A Land of Trouble

From a tall fire tower overlooking the village, you can see Dorset snuggling down in a tufted carpet of fir trees spreading beyond the horizon. The Central Ontario cousin of the ancient English county owes its naming to Thomas Gibbs Ridout, who became the Surveyor-General of what was then the Royal Province of Upper Canada. He was one of two sons of a Sherborne miller who both migrated to the New World in the eighteenth century. His elder brother, John, settled in Maryland, now a US State, and acquired riches, plantations, slaves, a society wife and a seat in the provincial government.

John and Thomas Gibbs Ridout were the sons of George Ridout, a tenant of the Digby family who acquired the Sherborne estate after Raleigh was condemned to death. George sent John, a pimply sixteen-year-old, to Oxford where, after five years' study and graduation, he received the invitation that was to determine the course of his life. It came from Colonel Horatio Sharpe who had served the army of the reigning George II at home and abroad and at the age of thirty-five was looking forward to a new career in Maryland. He had been appointed the next governor by the proprietor of the province, Frederick Calvert, the sixth and last Lord Baltimore, and now the tall, dignified soldier needed 'a scholar and a gentleman' to accompany him as his private secretary. Ridout was recommended to him, and the two embarked on the good ship *Molly*. After three months at sea, it breezed up the Chesapeake Bay that cleaves Maryland in two and in August 1753 dropped anchor off the capital, Annapolis.

If Ridout had expected a rough settlement of log cabins and homespun pioneers, he was to be reassured by a scene reminiscent of Weymouth back in his native Dorset. An established port lay in a curving harbour busy with sails. Alongside wharves and warehouses, bare-masted ships bore the national flags of Europe. The cries of stevedores echoed across the water as they unloaded the finest products from across the ocean and reloaded the principal source of Maryland's prosperity, tobacco. Ridout could see beyond the docks a well laid-out town of fine brick buildings and streets clattering with horse-drawn vehicles, among them carriages bearing fashionably-dressed ladies and gentlemen.

As Ridout and Sharpe came ashore members of the Upper House of the colony's legislating assembly gathered on the dock to greet their new governor. They were led by the Honourable Benjamin Tasker, who had been deputising as governor since the death of the previous incumbent, his wealthy son-in-law Samuel Ogle. Ogle's ten year old granddaughter, Mary, stood with the welcoming party watching the formal handshakes. Neither she nor Ridout were to know then, but the Dorset miller's son was seeing his future wife.

Ridout had arrived in a Maryland which only 120 years earlier had been wild territory, inhabited only by Indians with painted faces. The English emigrants sent by the colony's founder, the second Lord Baltimore, had been followed by many more, and now Maryland was earning a reputation as the most sophisticated of the British settlements in North America. The colony was a clone of eighteenth-century England, a stratified society in which the planters enjoyed a life of elegance and pleasure revolving around the sumptuous mansions built on the vast estates. The fashionable flocked to the racecourse and field sports in the countryside and to the social attractions of the town, the ballroom and the newly-opened theatre.

Beneath the glossy veneer was the sobering reality of class resentments that had been present from the beginning in a medieval system of land apportionment and official favouritism, which was increasingly dividing the Lower and Upper Houses of the Legislature. There was poverty and squalor among the underprivileged, not least the thousands of slaves brought from Africa and the convicts transported in chains from the mother country.

Beyond the domestic issues there were boundary quarrels with the neighbouring Virginia and Pennsylvania, fear of Indian raids on the frontier, and the perceived threat of invasion by the French. Sharpe, expected to perform the balancing act of governing the province in a fair and tolerant way and protecting the vested interests of his employer back in England, was later to write feelingly of 'a land of trouble'.

The current 'cold war' with France in the North American land-grab was spreading alarm among the British colonies bordering on the Allegheny Mountains. George II had claimed 500,000 acres of the rich Ohio Valley on the western side of the mountains, but the French were challenging with a southern push from Canada and had set up a heavily-armed fort in the valley. Virginia determined to warn the commander of the possible consequences of this action, and sent a small party of interpreters and backwoodsmen with an ultimatum. In charge of the 500 mile trek, through forest inhabited by Indians allied to the French, was a twenty-one year old militia major by the name of George Washington. Ridout was later to become a firm friend of the future first President of the United States.

The warning was ignored by the French, and a few months later, Washington was again despatched into the wilderness, this time in charge of 159 armed men. They built a British outpost called Fort Necessity in Western Pennsylvania, but had to surrender it to a combined force of French and Indians. The news of the defeat reached Sharpe in the summer of 1754, and with funds pledged by the Maryland assembly to help Virginia resist an invasion, he began gathering supplies. As commander-in-chief of the Maryland militia, he took charge of the volunteers swarming towards Fort Cumberland in the north of the colony where the Virginian forces under Washington, now twenty-two and a Lieutenant-Colonel, were establishing a line of defence.

Sharpe was acting with the military expertise that had commended him to Lord Baltimore, but he was obliged by rank to hand over to Major-General Edward Braddock, newly-arrived from European methods of warfare and scornful of the colonials' experience of frontier fighting. He set out to attack Fort Duquesne in Pennsylvania, confident that the French defenders would quail at the mere sight of his disciplined British regiments stiffening the militia. A small force of French and Indians sprang an ambush and routed Braddock's army. Out of 1,460 men, a total of 456 were killed or wounded. Washington had two horses shot from under him and was the only staff officer to survive the carnage. The foolish general was mortally wounded.

Ridout accompanied Sharpe to survey the gruesome scene where wagons, guns, ammunition and provisions were strewn about the ground. The artillery and £25,000 in cash had gone. The British abandoned Fort Cumberland, and thereupon the Indians fell on isolated farms, murdering and scalping, pillaging and razing, and putting the hard-won crops to the torch. The military disaster and the Indian terror caused consternation in Maryland.

Ridout was not paid for being the governor's private secretary, but in 1760 the governor appointed him a Customs officer for which he received £250 a year. Within three years he had made enough money to buy an estate in Anne Arundell County (named after the wife of the second Lord Baltimore). It was the first of several properties.

In 1756 Sharpe demonstrated his increasing dependence on Ridout by sending him to parley with the Indians. Sharpe had sensed an opportunity to drive a wedge between the French and their Indian allies following an unexpected letter from the Cherokee chief, Wahachy, expressing friendly feelings towards the British.

Ridout and a merchant named Daniel Wolstenholme, accompanied by a small posse of officers, were confronted in the wilderness about fifty miles from Annapolis by a fierce band of Indian warriors. They were Cherokees come to escort the deputation to the gate of Fort Frederick, which Maryland had set up in the vulnerable north-west of the province and named after the sixth Lord Baltimore.

Ridout and Wolstenholme were invited to smoke a pipe of peace with Wahachy. They realised the negotiations were going to be tough when the chief demanded to know where the presents were that he had been promised. He was told they were on their way. The chief then asked why Pennsylvania was holding talks with its enemies, the Shawnees and Delawares. He was told diplomatically that the talks were taking place only with those tribes who disapproved of their brothers' conduct and were 'in amity' with the British. Two Indian captives were then paraded before the Maryland delegates and obliged to sing 'death songs'.

The next day, a wagon arrived with the presents, and Ridout and his companion added £100 for the release of the two captives and for the scalps of four others who had been killed by Wahachey's braves. The chief replied that it was Indian custom and a matter of honour to preserve scalps taken in battle, but his obstinacy seemed

Thomas Ridout. (Robertson's
Landmarks of Toronto by
J. Ross Robertson)

to be mollified by the handover of a further £100 and more presents, and the
gruesome deal was done.

Ridout and Wolstenholme returned to Annapolis with the four scalps and
Wahachey's formal promise of support against the French. The two unfortunate
captives appear to have got lost in the translation.

Britain declared war on the French and began the domination of the colonial
scene, which led three years later to the Treaty of Paris and the ceding of America
and Canada to Britain, but it was not the end of French intervention, as the War of
Independence was to prove.

Benefiting from Sharpe's patronage, Ridout rose in social and political esteem
with appointments as Collector of Taxes, Deputy Secretary of the province, and
member of the assembly's Upper House, the King's Council.

At the age of thirty-two he was sufficiently established in the Maryland hierarchy
to be considered a fit husband for Mary Ogle, the child whom he had seen on his
arrival in Maryland and who was now a young woman of twenty-one. The marriage
must have been one of the great social occasions of 1764. For his bride, Ridout built
a house which is still among the handsomest in Annapolis. Subsequently he added
three attached houses on an adjoining plot.

It is likely that Washington was among the guests because of his friendship with Ridout. He stayed quite often at the Ridout residence during visits to Annapolis from his estate just over the Virginian border. Possibly another guest was Ridout's step-sister Elizabeth, who is known to have arrived from England in November 1963 and was in Annapolis in February the following year (Ridout's mother had died and his father married again).

In a letter she sent to England, Elizabeth relates that she danced with Washington to music played by Benjamin Franklin, another future US president. The instrument was devised by Franklin using mechanically-operated musical glasses and can be seen today in a Philadelphia museum.

Ridout played a prominent part in healing the boundary row which had festered between Maryland and Pennsylvania for many years, and in 1767 he was one of the signatories to the Mason-Dixon agreement. The 'Mason-Dixon Line' is popularly regarded today as separating the northern from the southern states of the USA.

Through his official duties, Ridout was concerned with the importation of hundreds of Africans. The appalling conditions they suffered crammed into slave-ships are graphically described in Alex Haley's bestselling book *Roots*, which became the basis of an acclaimed television programme. He tells how, during his research, he came across a newspaper advertisement in the *Maryland Gazette* of 1 October 1767 which announced the arrival at Annapolis of 'a cargo of choice healthy slaves' for sale at auction. Among those 'choice' slaves was Haley's ancestor, Kunta Kinte. One of the two authorising names at the foot of the advertisement is Ridout's.

Sharpe sailed for England in 1773 after fifteen years in the governor's seat and demonstrated his appreciation of Ridout's service to him in a practical way. He left the debts due to him and the sizeable interest on them to Ridout and appointed him to manage Whitehall, his plantation a few miles from Annapolis. Eight years later Sharpe sold him most of his property in Maryland, including the 650 acre Whitehall and two other plantations of 1,000 and 1,637 acres. With Whitehall went an imposing mansion with fine furnishings and works of art, lawns stretching down to the Chesapeake, livestock and thirty-four slaves. With Sharpe on the voyage to England was John's eldest son, Samuel, who was going to Harrow School.

Some accounts say the Ridout surname is an anglicised version of de Rideout, belonging to a French Huguenot family from Sance, near Fontainebleau. Apparently, it was brought across the Channel by a Thomas de Rideout fleeing the seventeenth-century 'Massacre of St Bartholomew', the infamous ethnic cleansing of Huguenot Protestants ordered by the twenty year old Charles II of France, under the baleful influence of his mother, Catharine de Medici. If this were true, it would have been the first time since the Norman invasion five centuries earlier that French was heard amid the homespun burr of Southwest England along the Somerset/Dorset border. It would have sounded strange to the shepherds, ploughboys, tradesmen and the like, though not perhaps to some of the educated clerics and gentry in the big houses. Sir Walter Raleigh, a previous Lord of Sherborne, would certainly have heard the language having fought in the Huguenot Army as a young man. The evidence for the story centres on a Thomas Ridout living at Henstridge on the Somerset side of the Dorset county border in 1551, who was granted a coat of arms by the College of Arms in London which bore a striking resemblance to that of the de Rideouts, but that is all, 'a striking resemblance'. There is also a will dated 1551 by a Walter Ridout of Langlin, Dorset, bequeathing a large sum of money to the church in Fontainebleau. William Ridout, of The Ridout Society, who has been researching the history of his tribe for many years, has seen the will, and found that it refers not to Fontainebleau but to Fontmell Manor, a village just a few miles from old Walter's home. The Huguenot Society in London was unable to find a de Rideout mentioned in England. So much for historical fact.

8

A Town Named Digby

The American War of Independence was going badly for the British in the summer of 1781. Canada was loyal to George III, but the Republican rebels were gaining ground in the south where an army of 8,000 British and Hessian troops was trapped in Virginia by a French/American force of twice their number. The British hold on the north was precarious, but strong in New York where the city's lifeline to the sea was being protected by the British North American Fleet. That August a new commander was appointed to take over the Fleet.

Rear-Admiral Robert Digby of Minterne Magna in Dorset was second-in-command of the Channel Fleet when the order came to sail to New York, and he arrived with his flagship, the ninety-gun *Prince George*, and three attendant warships just as preparations were being finalised for a second attempt to extricate the army besieged on the Yorktown Peninsular. Digby courteously stood aside to allow his predecessor, Admiral Thomas Graves, to keep command of the relief expedition, but when Graves approached the Virginia coast with his fleet and 3,000 British, Hessian and Loyalist troops on board, he found forty French warships blocking the way to the stricken army through the narrow entrance to Chesapeake Bay, and he wisely decided that any rescue bid would be doomed to failure. In any case it would have been futile; General Charles Cornwallis, with half his men sick or wounded, had surrendered.

Although the Yorktown setback and the advent of the French had turned the tide of the war in George Washington's favour, the British still had 30,000 soldiers in America, and as long as the king refused to treat with the revolutionaries, Digby and his command would continue through the winter of 1781–82 guarding the New York redoubt and patrolling for Yankee privateers preying on shipping outside the harbour.

On the New Jersey side of the Hudson River, the Americans were secretly plotting a commando raid that could win them the war. They planned to kidnap Digby and a 'Very Important Person' staying with him in his official residence in New York's Hanover Square. Four whale-boats would be rowed across the Hudson at the dead of night carrying about forty armed men with orders to overpower the sentry guards, smash their way into the building, which was easily identifiable by the monumental eagles on the gateposts, and snatch Digby and the VIP from their beds. The rebels hoped that such eminent hostages would attract a large ransom and persuade the obstinate monarch to sue for peace - the VIP was his own fifteen-year-old son, Prince William. Washington approved the plans and wrote in March 1782 to Colonel Ogden, commander of the American regiment:

> The spirit of enterprise so conspicuous in your plan for surprising, in their quarters and bringing off the Prince William Henry and Admiral Digby, merits applause, and you have my authority to make the attempt in any manner and at such a time as your judgement shall direct.

Washington laid it down that the two hostages must be treated with 'a proper line of conduct' and 'all possible respect' and conveyed to the revolutionary Congress in Philadelphia 'without delay'. Later his spies reported a stiffening of security in Hanover Square, and the plan was dropped.

Digby had been personally responsible for William for the past two years. The boy's parents had worried that he might be drawn into the drinking, gambling and womanising ways of his older brothers, the princes George and Frederick, and the king wondered whether a naval career might be a good character-building exercise for the lad. Digby assured him that it would; he was himself a good example to follow, a stern but fair disciplinarian noted for his all-round seamanship. He had entered the senior service at an early age, risen through command of a succession of ever-larger vessels, and fought in many actions off the French and Spanish coasts.

Digby was promoted to Rear-Admiral in June 1779, on the same day that Prince William, then thirteen, was piped aboard the *Prince George* at Portsmouth. Digby now had a future king of the British Empire in his complement, and his instructions were to see that the royal midshipman performed obediently every task he was given, learned every aspect of naval operations, and conducted himself politely, while his general education would be assured by his accompanying tutors. His first lesson in the reality of armed conflict at sea came within a few months. With mounting excitement the young prince watched the feverish preparations in the Channel Fleet to meet a French invasion armada of about 400 transports and thirty warships setting out for the England coast, but the 50,000 troops were suffering from sickness and a shortage of supplies and returned to France without a shot being fired.

In December, William experienced the full horror of war. Digby's ships were escorting a convoy of merchantmen with relief supplies for the lonely Gibraltar garrison when they were intercepted by a powerful squadron from Spain, which had allied itself with France. During the engagement the seventy-gun *Santo Domingo* was repulsed and blown up, with the loss of 600 lives. William wrote to his father, 'It was a most shocking and dreadful sight.' Standing by Digby's side, he watched as the *Prince George* loosed a broadside at the *Saint Julian,* and a boarding party was scrambled to take possession. The British flagship was slightly damaged by shot in the engagement, and seven crew members were wounded, one fatally.

The Spanish scattered, and five of their ships surrendered. On arrival at the Rock, Digby took William to a celebratory dinner with the governor, General Elliott, but it was not all over. Sailing back to England, Digby's fleet encountered the sixty-four-gun French warship *Prothée* shepherding three merchantmen, and all four were seized as prizes. William presented the colours of the *Prothée* and the *St Julian* to his father at a ceremony in England.

Digby predicted that his royal protégé would become 'a very great sea officer', but the boisterous youth was proving difficult to restrain. In Gibraltar he had been involved in a drunken brawl and but for Digby's intervention, would have appeared before the local magistrates. While on leave in London William resumed his association with his good-time brothers and became infatuated with a young woman. His father had feared such a situation and must have felt relieved when Digby had William back on board in January 1781. After yet another siege-breaking mission to Gibraltar, Digby crossed the Atlantic to assume his new command.

The king had insisted that William should become the first royal to set foot in America, although the young prince would not have been; the future Charles II, as the Duke of York, had led the army that took New Holland from the Dutch in 1600s.

All the same, the New World would get him away from the temptations of London society. But in the relative inactivity of New York the young Prince grew restless, and Digby recommended to the king that his son should return to the sea. Accordingly, William parted from Digby and embarked on what would become a distinguished naval career.

By the age of twenty he was a captain, but when promotion to Rear-Admiral was mooted in later years he fell out with Digby, who advised him against accepting the appointment, fearing that it could involve him in constitution politics and might damage his future career. Although William was offended by the remark, Digby declined to apologise. William was created Duke of Clarence in 1789 and rose to Lord High Admiral in the reign of his brother George IV, whom he eventually succeeded as William IV. His reputation as Britain's only really professional sailor king owed much to his mentor, the Dorset admiral Robert Digby.

As the stalemate dragged on in New York, a new governor, Lieutenant-General Sir Guy Carleton, arrived in 1782 bringing Digby the latest news of the political wrangles at home. The king still believed, despite the Yorktown disaster, that he was in the right in pursuing the American war, even though the intervention of France and Spain had made it a world war. There was some brighter news - Admiral Richard Howe had relieved Gibraltar against a formidable combination of French and Spanish ships, and in the Battle of the Saints in the West Indies, Admiral George Rodney decimated the French fleet which had prevented the Yorktown rescue. Even so, five years after the Declaration of Independence, opinion in the United Kingdom was veering ever stronger towards an accommodation with the republicans, and in May Carleton wrote to the American leader reporting his arrival and announcing that he was 'joined with Admiral Digby' in the commission of peace and most anxious to reduce the 'needless severities' of the war. Washington was sceptical about this hint of a negotiated settlement and remained so when another letter arrived four months later bearing Digby's signature, as well as Carleton's, and suggesting an exchange of prisoners. Despite the lukewarm response to these overtures, Digby told his captains that peace was 'not improbable' and warned them against destroying any prizes they took until the legal technicalities were sorted.

The war was formally ended on 3 September 1783 by the Treaty of Versailles, under which the United Kingdom recognised the independence of her American colonies, and they in turn acknowledged British sovereignty in Canada. France and Spain were guaranteed the integrity of their North American possessions, and the continent was solemnly shared among the four nations. The accord would prove to be fragile.

Digby had played a prominent role in the events that led to American independence. His last duty was to safeguard the 60,000 Loyalists who abandoned their homes in the incipient republic to seek new lives in Canada, the Maritimes, and the West Indies. Some returned to Britain. The great convoy sailed from New York in the autumn of 1783, protected from privateers by the navy led by Digby in *Atlanta*. Thousands of the refugees settled in Nova Scotia, a virtual island except for a narrow isthmus joining it to New Brunswick and the Canadian mainland, and the name of the town close to where hundreds landed was changed from Conway to Digby in honour of the admiral. In time the Nova Scotians became known as 'Blue Noses', stemming from the jibe in the land the refugees had left behind them that 'now the Loyalists have gone to such a cold place as Nova Scotia they carry their guilt in the middle of their faces!' As for Digby, he proceeded to the colony's capital, Halifax, and brought Sir Henry Clinton, commander in chief of the British land forces in America, and General Knyphausen, head of the Hessian contingent, back to Britain.

Digby's involvement in America had ended, and he came home to Minterne and the 1,548 acre estate he had bought from the Churchill family in 1765, bringing with him a widow he had met in New York. Mrs Eleanor Jauncey was the eldest daughter of a former vice-governor of the city, Andrew Elliott. She and the admiral were married by special licence, and despite their age difference – he was fifty-two and she was thought to be in her late thirties or early forties - it proved to be a loving union, although childless, and with affectionate humour he entered in his diary for 17 August 1800, 'On this day I have been married for 16 years and have never repented.'

The fourteenth-century village of Minterne Magna (Great Hintock in Thomas Hardy's pastoral novel *The Woodlanders*) sleeps on the country road that undulates across the billowing hills between Sherborne and the county town, Dorchester. Previously, the Digby estate had been rented for 135 years by a family whose name resounds through British history - the Churchills. The first Churchillian resident was a Winston Churchill who enlarged the original Elizabethan house. His younger son, General Charles Churchill, inherited the lease, and older son, John, was the Great Duke of Marlborough, who was acclaimed Britain's finest general after his victory over the French and Austrians at Blinden, known to the British as Blenheim. Winston's great Second World War namesake visited and admired Minterne on more than one occasion. During that war, Minterne House became a naval hospital and the Churchill and Digby dynasties were united by matrimony (see Chapter 16 A Legend in her Time). General Churchill's widow held Minterne until she died in a house fire in Dorchester, whereupon Digby bought the lease from the landlords, Winchester College, in 1768 with his share of the proceeds from the many prizes he and his men had captured at sea.

Digby disparaged his Minterne home as 'ill-contrived and ill-situated' and the grounds as 'compact but naked and the trees not thriving', but it had the overriding merit of nearness to his birthplace, Sherborne Castle, seven miles away which, despite its militaristic title, was a lively family residence presided over at that time by his brother Henry, the seventh Lord Digby. In his diary, which he kept in meticulous detail, the admiral recorded his happy times at the castle and recalled with affection the busy flow of visitors, the game shoots, the sailing in summer, and the skating fun on the lake in winter. He remembered an amusing occasion in January 1774 when he and his brother Charles, together with Lord Stavordale, 'pushed the Ladies in chairs on the ice'. The lake had been transformed from a couple of modest fishponds by Capability Brown, the famed architect and landscaper, who was making changes to bring the castle grounds into line with the prevailing fashion of other landed estates in the country. Digby modelled his ideas on Brown's design before commencing his own landscaping at Minterne, and he travelled widely looking at estates in England and the family property at Offaly in Ireland. Sailors made redundant when ships were laid up after the end of the American conflict helped him in the task of reshaping his estate. Carefully chosen trees and shrubs, many of them rare importations from the East, were planted in strategic locations, a tributary of the little River Cerne running through the estate was dammed to form a lake in the valley below the house, and fourteen cascades were constructed. He rolled up his own sleeves in the construction of the picturesque bridge which he later named the Lady Eleanor Bridge.

In his early years he had been 'very wild', according to the present Lord Digby, Edward Digby, but quickly proved his worth as a naval officer and was captaining a frigate by the age of twenty-four.

While away on duty he installed a housekeeper to look after the house at Minterne, an appointment that brought a scathing rebuke from a Mrs Cornwallis. In the imperious tones of a Lady Bracknell in Oscar Wilde's play *The Importance of Being Earnest,* she wrote:

> I hear you have a significant housekeeper, and this will not do. You may keep a mistress in one
> establishment and have a housekeeper in your home, but if you combine the two offices you

will force the poor girl to be dishonest because she must allow for the day that you will cast her off and therefore must cheat you for the bills etcetera.

There was no statutory industrial tribunal in those days to which the 'poor girl' could have appealed for compensation for unfair dismissal. In any case, her duties may have been rather more than just looking after the house; she is believed to have been the mother of Digby's two illegitimate children, Robert Murray and Robert Sherbourne. Murray followed the family tradition into the navy and rose to become an admiral. Robert, on the other hand, was an accomplished artist, and examples of his work appear in the picture gallery at Minterne House along with the valuable Churchill collection of portraits and tapestries which came with the purchase of the house. He managed a plate glass factory at St Helens in Lancashire which was established in 1773 and financed by his father. Based on a French invention, it was the first of its kind in England.

Digby senior was promoted to Vice-Admiral in 1787 and Admiral seven years later, shortly before his retirement. His care of the young Prince William ensured him a particular place in the royal affections, and in July 1801 he was present at George III's favourite seaside resort at Weymouth on the Dorset coast for the elaborate celebrations marking the king's recovery from a bout of porphyria, a recurring form of the insanity which finally killed him.

Admiral Sir Robert Digby, to give him his full title, died on 25 February 1815 at the age of eighty-two and rests in the company of members of the Churchill family whose monuments tend to overpower the simple wooden interior of the little church of St Andrew at the entrance to the leafy drive that winds up to Minterne House. When Eleanor died in 1830, Minterne passed to her husband's nephew, Henry Digby, who had followed the family's seafaring tradition and was an admiral.

Eighty-five years after Robert Digby's demise, dry rot condemned Minterne House to demolition, and around 1904 it was replaced by the present mansion, which reflects Gothic and Classic styles as well as Elizabethan. At one time fourteen staff were employed, but now the main part of the house is occupied by Lord and Lady Digby today, and the rest has been converted into apartments. The grounds are open to the public in aid of a national garden charity, and visitors can follow the same two miles of woodland paths that their creator and his wife had strolled.

Nova Scotia has never forgotten the Dorset sailor who safeguarded the newcomers' departure from New York and helped swell the British presence in a province which had been disputed with France until 1763 and still included French settlements. The Digby name occurs indelibly in the part of the colony where the Loyalist newcomers landed. The town of Conway was renamed Digby and so was the county of which it is the capital, and many other geographical features have followed suit. The colony's Admiral Digby Historical Society has published another reminder and an unusual one, the Digby Cookbook. Dedicated to the Digby Lobster Fleet, which operates out of Digby Harbour, it contains such enticing recipes as Digby King Scallops, Digby Scallop Burger, Digby Scallop Turnovers,

Digby Seafood Salad, Digby Delight, Digby Pizza, Digby Scallop Kabobs, Digby Scallop Dip, Baked Digby Scallops, Digby Pie, Digby Baked Scallops and Haddock, and Grilled Digby Scallops. Surely, no other British admiral has earned such appetising fame!

How the Stamp Act Came Unstuck

In June 1788 Digby went to see the Prime Minister who had been at the centre of the notorious legislation that cost Britain its American colonies. The third Earl of Bute, otherwise Lord Stuart of Rothesay, lived in a cliff-top mansion overlooking Christchurch Bay, about forty miles from Minterne Magna. He had been chosen by George III to lead his government because he was a friend and could be trusted while political wrangling was dividing the nation. From the moment of his appointment, Bute resorted to bribery and corruption to push the king's fiscal ambitions through a reluctant Parliament. The monarch was adamant that the colonies should pay towards their defence, but he also needed more cash from the home country, and Bute was expected to find it with a proposed tax on cider. A rise in the price of a favourite beverage proved too much for the public to swallow, and angry mobs stoned Bute's carriage in the London streets. Britain's most hated Prime Minister was forced to quit after only a year in office.

His successor, Lord North, pressed on with the proposed Stamp Act which required the use of specially stamped paper for documents of various kinds, but the colonials reacted so violently that this notorious tax was dropped - only to be replaced by a levy on tea which proved even more distasteful to the consumers. One night fifty rebels disguised as Mohawk Indians boarded three ships newly arrived from Britain and dumped their cargoes of tea into Boston harbour. The 'Boston Tea Party', as history recalls the incident, was a precursor of rising disaffection with the Crown which exploded in the War of Independence.

Bute never fully recovered from his political defeat but found some solace in a love of botany which drew him through the flora of the New Forest to Christchurch Bay, where he fell under the spell of the spectacular views out to sea. He engaged the noted architect Robert Adams to design him a mansion with thirty bedrooms and stabling for ten horses, but while his noble sanctuary gave him a new lease of life it may have contributed to his demise. Reportedly, he fell while climbing on the cliffs and was nursing his wounds in his London home when he died in 1792. The seaside mansion was pulled down. The land was sold but bought back some years later by a grandson, Charles Stuart, who built a stately retirement home a safer distance from the crumbling cliffs. With the grandiose title of Highcliffe Castle, it incorporates many fine examples of medieval French masonry and stained glass which Charles collected during a long and eventful career in the diplomatic service. One of Dorset's, indeed England's, finest examples of romantic-picturesque architecture, the castle was rescued from near-ruin in recent years.

If Digby had met the acquisitive diplomat's father, another Charles and one of Lord Bute's eleven children, a very lively discussion might have transpired during his visit. This son, like the admiral, had served in the American war for four years with the Cameronian Regiment and emerged as a Lieutenant-Colonel. He was a fierce critic of the blundering British leadership which he described as 'disgraceful', and foresaw how the war would end. One wonders how Digby would have responded.

9

Shipbuilder Launches Hospital for Waifs

Although he had given up the construction of sailing ships in Massachusetts and was now a prosperous shipping merchant in eighteenth-century London, Dorset-born Thomas Coram never lost faith in the New World and devoted his life to promoting its future, but one day an added concern entered his life. While walking between his home and office in the city centre he chanced upon the body of a baby lying discarded in a filthy street. Tough man of the world though he was, Coram was sickened by the plight of this tiny waif and vowed to set up a refuge for illegitimate children. At that time an estimated 1,000 were being abandoned every year in the streets of the capital by mothers too poor, too ill, or too ashamed to keep them. Privileged society was largely ignoring the poverty around it, and seventeen years passed before Coram's dogged persistence finally won the funds and support he needed from the moneyed and influential. The Hospital for the Maintenance and Education of Exposed and Deserted Young Children, the Foundling Hospital, opened its doors on 25 March 1741 - and desperate mothers with pathetic bundles were already queuing outside.

The bluff seafarer with a soft heart for the underprivileged had led an eventful life on both sides of the Atlantic. He was born in the small port of Lyme Regis on the Dorset coast in 1668, but little is known or even sure about his early days, except that his father, John Coram, had moved the family from the neighbouring county of Somerset in search of work and secured a job as a seaman (or, some say, customs man) at Lyme. There are two defining dates, and although no record of his own baptism has come to light, that of his younger brother William was recorded in 1671, and also the date of their mother's death on 13 September 1677 when Thomas was nine years old and the lone survivor of her four children. He was brought up by his father and, at the age of eleven and a half, was sent to sea in the tradition of the local lads and spent the next five years learning the seaman's rough trade under the canvas sails of merchant vessels plying Lyme harbour. When his father remarried and moved the family home to London, Thomas was apprenticed to a shipwright on the Thames. On the expiry of his apprenticeship in 1692, he was employed for some months checking the cargoes of ships sailing from England to Ireland, and for bringing in some extra income, Liverpool awarded him the honorary Freedom of the City.

At the age of twenty-five, he took a company of craftsmen to Massachusetts with the backing of a group of London businessmen and established a shipyard at the capital, Boston. The venture prospered under his practical experience as a shipwright, and its success encouraged him to open a new yard about forty miles away on a bank of the river at Taunton, where suitable ships' timber was readily available in the woods. The new yard built five ships in the next three years and introduced an innovative system of construction, launching one ship fully rigged rather than as a hull to be completed afloat. Even though he had brought a thriving new industry, he experienced hostility from the more extreme Puritan faction in Taunton. Their animosity towards his staunch Anglican faith led to difficulties with his material supplies, broken contracts, and lawsuits, including one which alleged slander and cost him his shipyard, two vessels and the home he had built. He appealed successfully against the slander verdict and, by way of damages, was awarded the fifty-nine acre estate of the man named Burt who had brought the action.

Afterwards Burt twice tried to shoot him and physically assaulted him on another occasion, which was strange behaviour for a deputy sheriff whose duty it was to uphold the law. Given the prevalent anti-Anglican feeling in the area, it is perhaps unsurprising that the revengeful assailant was never charged.

Coram drew no profit from the appropriated estate. Instead, by a deed of 8 December 1703, he offered the fifty-nine acres for the foundation of Taunton's first Episcopalian church and school, should the townsfolk ever become 'more civilised', as he put it. However, they chose to build their church elsewhere, and after his death the land, which had been put in trust, was sold and the proceeds given to rebuilding the church. Nevertheless, he was magnanimous when brazenly asked for a donation towards the building of the church, and he gave a rather special Book of Common Prayer for the use of the clergy. The book had been presented to him by a firm friend, Arthur Onslow, who was the Speaker of the House of Commons, a Privy Councillor, and Treasurer of the Royal Navy. Coram also helped to establish a parish library with a large gift of books which is treasured today, but the Nonconformist bigots of Taunton remained less than enthusiastic about his benevolence. The lawsuits started all over again, and one of his ships was seized. By 1702, Coram had had enough of the rancour and returned to Boston, although Taunton continued building ships for many years. In later years the town redeemed itself by naming a street after him and dedicating its Episcopal Church to St Thomas in his honour. Two years later and deep in debt, Coram sailed back to England with Eunice Wayte, whom he had married four years earlier. She was the eldest daughter of a prominent Boston couple, John and Eunice Wayte, who were members of the Congregational movement, which thought less unkindly of the Church of England. Their daughter had inherited their Nonconformist beliefs, yet despite the sectarian divide between her and her stubbornly Anglican husband, they enjoyed forty happy, though childless, years together.

He was in his forties when he set up in business in London as a merchant dealing with shippers and captains. Despite his own failure in the New World, he never gave up his interest or his faith in the opportunities it offered, and in the 1720s he took out a group of ex-servicemen and other would-be settlers to cultivate a strip of unsettled land in Maine, which the French had surrendered along with Nova Scotia under the 1720 Treaty of Utrecht which ended the War of Spanish Succession. Unfortunately for his plans, Massachusetts was awarded Maine, its northern neighbour, and he encountered the same animosity as before. Whether or not the greatest impediment was his sometimes tactless impatience and outspoken cussedness when opposed, there were disputes over the ownership of the land, and after seven years of trying he felt obliged to shelve the project.

Even so, he never forgot the scope for settlement in North America and gave active support to British government legislation which would benefit the colonies by reason of an Act designed to break Sweden's monopoly of the timber trade in favour of less expensive products from the coniferous forests of Carolina and its southern neighbour, Georgia. As well as saving the nation a great deal of money in the construction and maintenance of Royal Navy sailing ships, Coram saw Georgia as an opening for the poor and unemployed to make a new life for themselves and their families, and he was among the trustees supporting an application for a Royal patent that would raise the province to colony status. Wealthy merchants recognised a good commercial investment and subscribed £2,000 towards the cost of the application by a philanthropic soldier, General James Edward Oglethorpe (see Chapter 5 – Lord in a Manor of Speaking). On 12 April 1732, George II granted the founding charter to General Oglethorpe who was concerned to offer carefully selected debtors and ex-servicemen a home and a chance to make a good living in Georgia.

In November Coram watched the first settlers sail off to a promising future in the New World. It was a satisfying moment for the trustees, but within two years Coram had fallen out with the others – perhaps predictably, in view of his abrasive temper. He had sided with the complaints of the Georgia settlers that the fifty acres granted to each man carried the feudal restriction that the land may be inherited only by a male heir, to the exclusion of widows and daughters, and the men worried that an owner without a son could lose his hard-won property. But Coram's sympathy was outvoted by the other trustees, and his attendance at their meetings withered and eventually died.

His appetite for promoting British settlement in America was unassuaged, however, and by now he had influential friends in high places. His Maine project had ended in failure, but there was Nova Scotia, a virtual island off the coast which had been settled by the French. Coram disliked the French and the Catholic religion in equal measure, and sought royal assent to upgrade Nova Scotia from a province to a British, and therefore Anglican, colony. He attached a petition signed by 102 artisans who had difficulty finding jobs in Britain, but again his colonising efforts failed, although the history of the Coram Foundation published in 1935 recorded that the eventual settlement of Nova Scotia might have come later than 1749 had it not been for the Dorset mariner. His interest in the New World also extended to the agitation in support of the Native Americans who had been defrauded over the purchase of their lands for settlement.

Following the accession of the Hanoverian Elector George I to the British throne in 1714, Coram saw an opportunity to break the Scandinavian monopoly on ship materials for the Royal Navy, and in 1720 he lobbied Parliament to lift the ban on imports from Germany. He embarked on an attempt to encourage potential German suppliers and sailed on the merchantman *Sea Flower* bound for Hamburg, but the ship ran aground in the River Elbe estuary at Cuxhaven and fell foul of plunderers from local communities. They proceeded not only to steal its cargo of wheat but to tear the vessel apart for its timber. Both Coram and the ship's master were assaulted and threatened with death, but they escaped ashore and Coram met the German authorities in Hamburg. The result of his enterprise was the repeal by Parliament of the ban on German imports and a consequent fall in the Scandinavian prices to the Royal Navy.

All this while the indefatigable philanthropist had continued seeking support for his 'darling project' as he called the charitable institution he founded to rescue the illegitimate children thrown on to the streets of London, many of them sick and dying. However, it was a time of financial crisis, and he was knocking on a reluctant door. Apart from other problems, Parliament had given the South Sea Company a monopoly on British commerce with America and other parts of the world, an activity that included the lucrative slave trade and the hope of discovering the mythical El Dorado that had eluded Raleigh, but its shares had been grossly oversold to a greedy public, and when the notorious South Sea Bubble burst, most of the deluded hopefuls were badly hit. Consequently, money and humanitarian sentiment were tight, and Coram found no titled aristocrat or senior churchman willing to support his petition to the king. As he afterwards wrote to a friend in his usual blunt manner, he might just as well have asked them 'to putt down their Breeches and present their Backsides to the King and Queen in a full Drawing room'.

The street-children of London were still suffering, and he was moved by the example of an established project for Parisian waifs which had discovered that if powerful men would not listen, perhaps their ladies could unlock that stubborn indifference.

In France the cunning stratagem worked, and it did in Britain when, on 9 March 1729, the compassionate Duchess of Somerset became the first to sign his petition. Over the next six years she was followed by twenty other noblewomen, including seven duchesses and eight countesses, and then came the men - dukes and earls, eminent physicians, prosperous merchants, Justices of the Peace, Members of Parliament, and the Archbishop of York breaking the previous reluctance of the church. Some of the males were related to the female signatories, and Coram later acknowledged that without the petticoat pressure he would not have obtained that precious Royal Charter.

Right: 1 Portrait of Sir Walter Raleigh, by the artist William Segar, 1598. (National Gallery of Ireland, Dublin, The Bridgeman Art Gallery)

Below: 2 In quest of El Dorado, Sir Walter Raleigh led an expedition to find the city in 1595, which advanced 300 miles up the Orinoco River into Guiana. (Bridgeman/British Library, London)

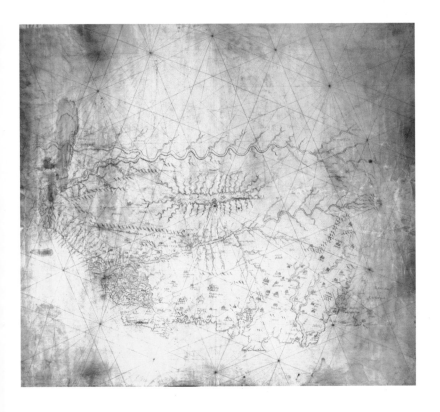

Opposite above left: 3 Anthony Ashley Cooper, 2nd Earl of Shaftsbury, by the artist Gerard Soest. (Agnew's, London, UK/The Bridgeman Art Gallery)

Opposite above right: 4 The Earl of Clarendon, Lord High Chancellor, by the artist Sir Peter Lely. (Middle Temple, London, UK/The Bridgeman Art Gallery)

Opposite below: 5 The old house, shipyard and outhouses at Trinity, Newfoundland, by Michael Corne. (The Dorset Natural History & Archaelogical Society, The Dorset County Museum)

This page: 6 Portrait of Thomas Coram by the artist William Hogarth. (Reproduced by kind permission of The Foundling Museum, London)

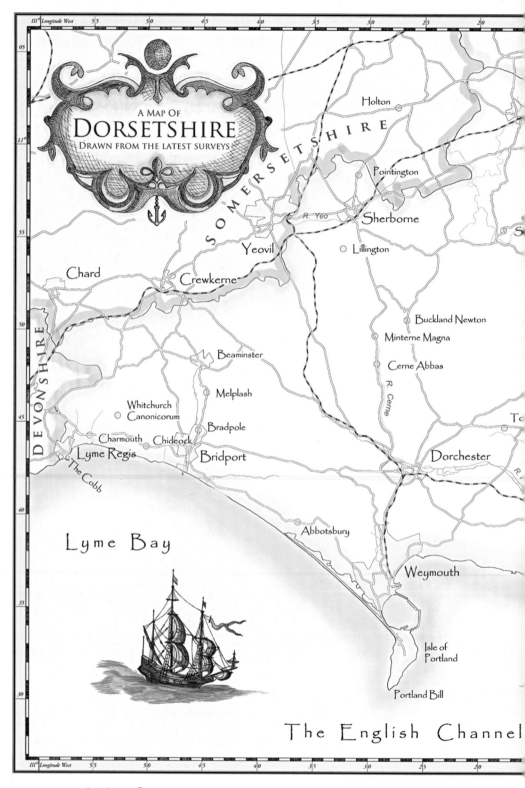

A MAP OF

DORSETSHIRE

DRAWN FROM THE LATEST SURVEYS

S O M E R S E T S H I R E

Holton

Pointington

R. Yeo

Sherborne

Yeovil

Lillington

Chard

Crewkerne

Buckland Newton

Minterne Magna

Cerne Abbas

Beaminster

R. Cerne

Melplash

Whitchurch
Canonicorum

Bradpole

Charmouth   Chideock

Lyme Regis

Bridport

Dorchester

The Cobb

Lyme Bay

Abbotsbury

Weymouth

Isle of
Portland

Portland Bill

The English Channel

D E V O N S H I R E

III° Longitude West

www.visit-dorset.com

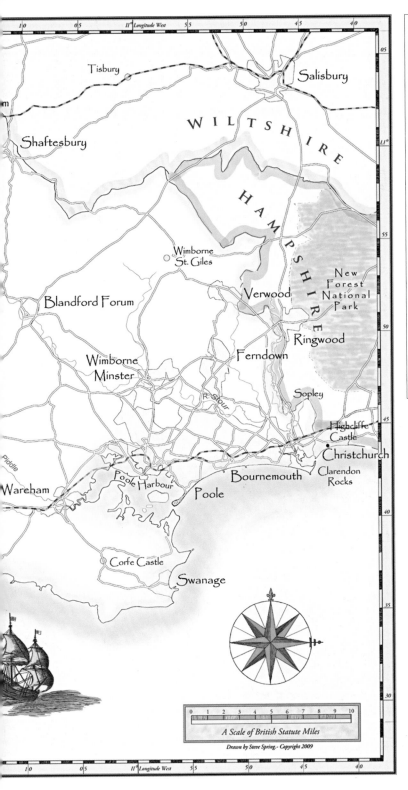

Dorset, one of the maritime counties of southern England, nestles between Devon, Somerset, Wiltshire and Hampshire.

Dorset is frequently described as being 'the best of both worlds', for behind a varied coastline that includes England's first World Heritage Site, lies a county rich in archaeology, unspoilt rural villages and countryside with a history to be proud of.

The county's first name was recorded in 940 AD and originates from the West Saxon settlers who made their home in the Roman town of Dorchester, now the county town.

7 A map of Dorset, incorporating the 1974 County Boundary changes, drawn from the latest surveys. (Created by Steve Spring, GIS Manager for Dorset County Council)

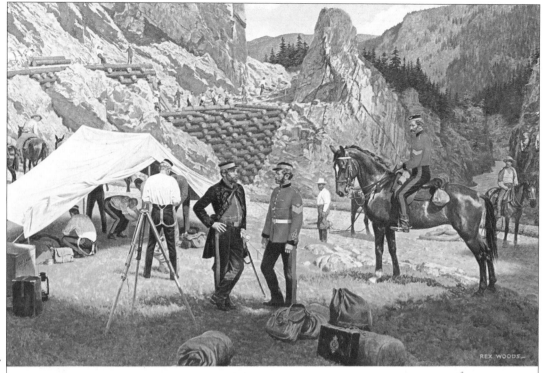

Above: 8 The Cariboo Road by Rex Woods. (Reproduced by kind permission of Rogers Communications Inc.)

Left: 9 A portrait of Robert Digby, by the artist Sir Joshua Reynolds. (Reproduced by kind permission of Mr John Wingfield Digby, Sherborne Castle)

Opposite above: 10 The Digby family on the steps of Minterne Magna. Pamela, the future US Ambassador to France, is second from the right. (Getty Images)

Opposite below: 11 Pamela Churchill Harriman, in the official capacity as US Ambassador to France. (Getty Images)

Pamela Harriman Foreign Service Fellowships program, based at the College of William and Mary in Virginia, was established in her legacy to inspire the best of a new generation to pursue careers in public service. 'It is you, the young people just entering public service, to whom we look to forge new paths of understanding among the nations of the World.'

Pamela Churchill Harriman

Left: 12 Reverentially, President Chirac placed on the US flag draped over the coffin a purple cushion bearing the scarlet sash and gold medal of the Grand Cross of the Legion of Honour. The English girl from rural Dorset had become the first American woman to receive France's highest honour. (Orban Thierry/Corbis Sygma)

Below: 13 President Bill Clinton, eulogising Pamela Churchill Harriman at a memorial service at Washington National Cathedral. (Wally McNamee/ Cobis)

Valuable backing also came from fashionable artists of the day, recruited by a friend and fellow childless philanthropist, William Hogarth. Among other painters to donate their works were Gainsborough and Francis Hayman. The latter's famous *Moses in the Bullrushes* shows an abandoned baby looking chubby and cared-for. Perhaps it was hoped the poignant contrast would draw public attention to the condition of the neglected street-children, or perhaps it was just catering for the public taste of the time, but Hogarth knew poverty at first hand. As a child he had been locked in the grim Fleet Street debtors prison with the other members of his family when their father was declared insolvent. Hogarth painted a realistic full-length portrait showing Coram dressed unaffectedly as was the old seaman's custom. Another benefactor was the German-born composer Georg Friedrich Handel who wrote an anthem for the hospital, held annual benefit performances of his *Messiah*, and donated an original score of the oratorio. The paintings and many other memorabilia can be seen in today's Foundation Museum, where the story is told of Thomas Coram and his continuing charity, not only Britain's first hospital created for 'foundlings', but also Britain's first public gallery space for the display of art.

King George II was sympathetic, gave £2,000 to the cause, signed the charter on 14 August 1739, and the hospital, for which the Lyme Regis seafarer had striven for nearly two decades of his life against indifference and some ridicule, was on its way. Although Coram was now over seventy, recovering from a long illness and mourning the death of his beloved Eunice in July 1740, he still had a lot of work to do, walking up to ten and twelve miles a day seeking subscriptions and enlisting members for the governing board. Finally, before an audience of 170 supporters, six dukes and eleven earls among them, he formally presented his hard-won charter to the Duke of Bedford, whom the governors had invited to be the president of the hospital. A large London house was leased and suitably adapted, staff were appointed, and on 25 March 1741, the first twenty children were admitted to the new Hospital for the Maintenance and Education of Exposed and Deserted Young Children, as it was known then, a term later altered to 'Foundling Hospital' to cover older children. By 8 May, sixty children had been saved from the streets. No questions were asked about their origins, but they had to pass two severe restrictions: they must not be over two months old or suffering from an infectious disease. The hospital was a place of hospitality, not a place to be cured.

As places were limited, mothers bringing their babies took part in a lottery. Drawing a white ball from the bag meant 'only to be admitted on the failure of a "white ball baby" to pass the medical'. A mother drawing a black ball meant 'not to be admitted', and were directly escorted to the hospital gates, hence the expression 'blackballed'. The treatment was strict and severe, but the hospital's fame quickly spread, and at times as many as a hundred desperate mothers with babes in their arms were fighting with each other in the scramble to reach the street door. The babies were baptised in the hospital, and by the nature of their birth they needed names. Numbers of youthful Bedfords, Marlboroughs, Montagues and other notables were eventually deemed fit for the outside world, along with Wycliffes and Latimers, Chaucers and Shakespeares, Drakes and Cromwells, and Vandykes and Hogarths. Appropriately, the first boy to be baptised in the hospital was named Thomas Coram and the first girl Eunice Coram; the names of the founder and his wife were later given to other children, and one of the Thomas Coram's is recorded as doing so well as a grown-up that he would visit the Foundation in his own carriage. In fact, on discharge most of the boys were destined for the sea or the armed forces and the girls became domestic servants.

By modern standards the living conditions in the hospital were austere and stiffly disciplined. As recently as 1914 one of the pupils placed in the care of foster parents recalled that when she was returned to the Foundling Hospital at the age of five, her hair was shaved off, presumably for reasons of hygiene, she was dressed like all the other girls in the regulation serge frock and apron, and a name-tag was hung around her neck. For one peccadillo, she was taken over a nurse's knee and slapped with a shoe. She was not a neglected child like most of the others, but was never told her true name and did not learn her family history until later in life. It turned out that her mother had been engaged to a soldier who had died of tuberculosis before they could be married. In desperation she handed her baby to the care of the Foundation. That child, who grew up to be the author of a book, *Recollections*, published by the Thomas Coram Foundation, which recalls how boys and girls were segregated; at mealtimes they were marched into the dining hall like soldiers, required to sit on wooden benches at the table and eat silently, and summoned to their feet at the sound of a gavel. Misdemeanours were answered with canings. But life wasn't all grey and institutionalised; she remembered with affection the summer camps, the concerts, and the music, adding 'we were brought up with Handel; at Christmas we always learnt the *Messiah*.'

The Lyme Regis sailor/captain whose own beginnings were obscure had given life to a London institution which was the first of its kind in Britain. His hospital was inundated with thousands of unwanted babies from outside London, and by the year 1760, branches had been established in other parts of the country. Meanwhile, he had been continuing his commercial dealings with ship owners and arranging the finance for their cargoes, but his charitable obsession had taken toll of the time demanded by his business, and his own purse was under strain. He was helped financially by friends and supporters – the Prince of Wales came up with a twenty guineas annuity – but he was a virtual pauper living in lodgings when he died on 29 March 1751 in his eighty-fourth year.

He was buried beneath the altar in the Foundation's chapel as he had wished. A memorial stone records that he died 'poor in Worldly Estate, rich in Good Works'. His bones have been moved several times and are now in St Andrew's Church in Bloomsbury since the old hospital was demolished in 1926. Among the most moving epitaphs to the humble seaman are the words on the memorial stone:

A man eminent in that most eminent virtue, the love of Mankind, little attentive to his private fortune, and refusing many opportunities of increasing it, his time and thought were continually employed in endeavours to promote the public happiness, both in this kingdom and elsewhere, particularly in the colonies of North America, and his endeavours were many times crowned with the desired success.

The Foundling Hospitals moved to Redhill in 1926, and in 1935 became a residential school in Berkhamsted, just outside London. Along with the move have come changes. The Thomas Coram Foundation, now a registered charity simply called Coram, works with vulnerable children, young people and their families, transforming their lives through practical help and support. Services today include: adoption, parenting and family support services, housing for care leavers and young people at risk and extended school services. The present staff are trained professional teachers, the children are treated with kindly devotion and respect, and there are summer camps, concerts and cycle rides in the surrounding countryside.

The humble seaman from Lyme who had revolutionised the social fabric of Britain in his lifetime and played a leading role in the founding of a southern US state is arguably the town's most celebrated son. Two years before he died his hometown honoured him with the Freedom of the Borough, and in a letter thanking the mayor and corporation he wrote that he would 'gladly embrace every good opportunity to justify my grateful knowledgements for their generous favour'.

Rather clumsy English, and he always admitted that because of his early education he was not much of a scholar, but thanks to him thousands of children and England's oldest children's charity have benefited from the level of good education and protected upbringing that he himself had been denied.

Coram's Fields, a children's playground, is at 93 Guildford Street, London, WC1N 1DN. Adults are only permitted if accompanied by a child.

The Foundling Museum is at 40 Brunswick Square, London, WC1N 1AZ
www.foundlingmuseum.org.uk.

Further information on The Thomas Coram Foundation for Children, a charity established by Royal Charter in 1739, can be found at www.coram.org.uk

10

Fish Were the Lure

In the eighteenth century, Newfoundland was still contributing to the prosperity it had brought to Dorset ports by reason of the teeming cod their fishermen were bringing back from the Grand Banks. The colonisation of Newfoundland had arisen 400 years earlier from Henry VII's eagerness to raise England's standing among the maritime nations of Europe. The king had not been persuaded by letters from Christopher Columbus seeking support for the theory that he could find a quicker, easier route to the riches of the Far East by sailing west across the Atlantic rather than south around Africa and then east across the Indian Ocean, but after learning that Columbus, with the backing of England's Spanish rival, had discovered what the mariner believed was the coast of China, the king acted and commissioned another Italian explorer, John Cabot, to take the English flag in the same westerly direction on condition that a fifth of any diamonds, gold or other treasure he found should go into the royal purse. Cabot (real name Giovanni Caboto) left Bristol in the spring of 1497 heading westward with the 70ft-long *Matthew* and a crew of eighteen, and two months later sighted what he thought, like Columbus five years before, was Asia. In fact, they had reached America.

What Cabot saw was Newfoundland and a coastal sea brimming with cod in shoals so dense they impeded the progress of his ship, and he reported on his acclaimed return to Bristol that his crew could pull the fish on board with baskets. This was not the sort of treasure to bring an immediate glint to the royal eye, and the intrepid sailor's reward for his achievement was a modest £10. The fishermen of south-west England were tempted to dare the hazards of the Atlantic, however, and over the years their catches transformed the economies of Dorset's three main ports Poole, Weymouth and Lyme Regis. Until the sixteenth century these modest communities had been engaged with fishing the less distant waters of the North Sea and Iceland, and on their outward journeys they carried local products to other parts of England, the Channel Islands and Brittany, particularly wool from the county's large flocks of sheep. Newfoundland cod were being landed in Poole, the largest of the Dorset ports, as early as 1528, and it is a measure of how the trade flourished that Poole's fishing fleet swelled from twenty-one to 230 ships and 1,500 men over the next sixty years. Comparable increases occurred at Weymouth and Lyme Regis. In time, a lively two-way traffic developed as a result of the permanent

The brig *Superb*, built in Poole around 1825, entering Naples Harbour loaded with salt cod from Newfoundland. (Poole Museum Service)

fishing settlements which the English and their French rivals established on the distant land. The boats that brought the salted and dried cod returned with English goods needed by the settlers; in the case of Dorset it was linen and woollen products, fishing nets and lines, rope and canvas. Home consumers found the hard, crispy fish unpalatable, and some of it ended up in Jamaica to feed the slaves on the sugar plantations. But much went to markets in Continental Europe where it was more appreciated, especially in Spain, Portugal and Italy, and the boats brought back wine, exotic fruit and other foreign goods for sale in eager markets at home.

For the crews, risking their lives in small boats on the turbulent ocean, it was tough, dirty, smelly work that demanded constant recruits or 'apprentices', as they were called. Some were boys as young as eleven and twelve from pauper hostels in Wimborne Minster, Christchurch and other local towns. The residents must have welcomed this opportunity to ease the drain on the parish finances, and the overseers perhaps felt relieved to unload their burden on the fishing boats of Poole.

Meanwhile, Poole became one of the wealthiest towns on the south-west coast of England. The merchants and fleet owners waxed extremely rich and powerful and built sumptuous mansions which survive in the area to this day. Prominent among the merchants were the Kemp family whose ancestry was traced back as far as the Norman conqueror, Duke William, by a genealogist descendant, George Ward Kemp, in *Kemps of Ollantigh and Kemps of Poole* published in Seattle in 1939. The *Ollantigh* in the title refers to the extensive family manor in the county of Kent. As well as having royal ties, the Kemps can boast a Bishop of London, a

Bishop of Canterbury who was twice Lord Chancellor and, through the female line, blood links with the crowns of England and Scotland. To their Kentish estates the Kemps added land in Dorset and the neighbouring county of Hampshire. The Kemp-Welch branch of the family acquired its hyphenation under a royal licence to add Welch to the surname in 1795. In addition to their other interests, the Kemps were bankers in Christchurch and settled themselves into the local landed gentry with the purchase of Sopley Manor and mansion just outside the town in 1868. By 1830 the bonanza was ebbing away; the Newfoundland settlers were finding new markets for their fish on the American mainland and in the Caribbean, and the New Englander fishermen were competing for the trade.

In the nineteenth century, the Kemp dynasty played a contributory role in the early development of the United States. In 1828 a George Kemp and his wife Elizabeth, née Miller, emigrated from Poole to America with their children. The parents died at Augusta in Michigan in 1863 (he was seventy-nine), and the children moved to various parts of North America. A daughter married a prominent businessman and banker who became Mayor of Rochester in New York State and built a Presbyterian Church. Her brothers Alfred, William, Arthur, and Henry, who had all been born in Poole, served in the Union Army during the Civil War that finally settled the independence of the United States from their homeland. Alfred left his home on a farm in Nebraska and served as a sergeant under General Custer, the general who was one of the slain in the notorious massacre carried out by Cheyenne Indians, led by Chief Sitting Bull. Alfred was later wounded with the cavalry on the blood-soaked plains at Gettysburg in the decisive battle of the Civil War. William and Arthur served in the Union Army in the Indian Wars of 1861-1870, and Arthur was an officer in the Union Army in the Civil War. According to the published history, the youngest son, Henry, was rejected by the army. It was said that because of his bad teeth he could not bite off the end of the heavy paper that enclosed the rifle cartridges of those days.

By the late 1830s the Dorset fishing trade with the Falklands began to falter under increasing competition from the American mainland and Newfoundland's own fishermen. Inevitably, after 300 years of intensive fishing, the fish stocks were becoming exhausted, and in 1992 the Canadian government put a total ban on the Grand Banks.

Who was Cabot?

The adventurous sea captain whose sighting of Newfoundland brought prosperity to the ports of Dorset was born Giovanni Caboto in the Italian port of Genoa in 1450. He settled in England with his family as a merchant in Bristol and anglicised his and other names; his ship, *Matthia* (his wife's name) became *Matthew*. He made three voyages to North America, venturing south along the coast from Labrador and exploring the island of Newfoundland and the near-island connected to the mainland by a narrow isthmus, Nova Scotia. On the second voyage he planted the English flag on Cape Breton Island off the Nova Scotian coast, where a bust has been erected showing him gazing out across the ocean that had brought prosperity to Dorset.

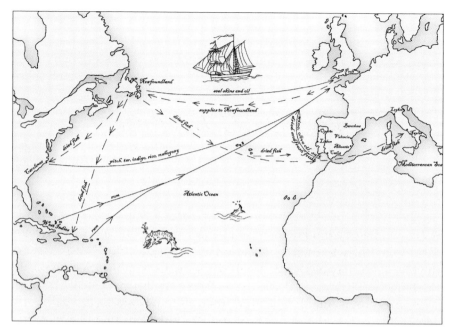

Typical trade routes of the Poole Merchants. (Poole Museum Service)

It was Sir Humphrey Gilbert, during his search for the Northwest Passage as an alternative route to the riches of the Asian continent around the Arctic coast of Canada, who formally claimed Newfoundland for England in 1583. Gilbert drowned on his way home when his frigate *Squirrel* capsized.

Cabot is credited with discovering New Jersey, which was initially settled by the Dutch but founded as an English colony in 1664 by Sir George Carteret, one of the eight proprietors of the Carolinas (see Chapter 6 The Earls and the Carolinas). Cabot is also credited with 'discovering' Newfoundland, but in fact archaeologists and historians have uncovered evidence that Norsemen from Greenland had visited the island, and before them native Inuits from the American mainland had established settlements. All the same, Cabot unwittingly opened the door to a warm and thriving relationship between Newfoundland and Dorset. The island and the English county are officially 'twinned', and Poole town enjoys a Friendship Agreement with the island's capital, St John's. A regional organisation, the Wessex Newfoundland Society, was set up many years ago and helped organise the June 1997 celebrations for the 500th anniversary of Cabot's landing, for which a replica of Cabot's ship sailed from Bristol to Newfoundland. A derelict house built by Poole fish merchants from the Lester family at Trinity on the Newfoundland coast in the eighteenth century was formally reopened as a museum after a £500,000 restoration programme. A descendant by marriage, John Bingley Garland, had rebuilt the house in 1821. He was a former Mayor of Poole and the first Speaker of the island's House of Assembly. The original dwelling is believed to have been the first brick-built house in North America - and the bricks came from Dorset.

11

'We WILL Be Free!'

The law-abiding Methodist communities in southern Ontario might have been alarmed had they learned the secret of the five family men who joined them from the English county of Dorset in the 1840s, but the truth reached Canada only after their deaths. They never disclosed to their neighbours that they and a sixth farm worker had been convicted as criminals in England and transported in chains to Australia. They were the innocent victims of a flagrant injustice that led to a national outcry and an estimated 50,000 protestors marching through the streets of the capital. The government was bombarded with petitions, and angry questions were asked in Parliament, until eventually a reluctant royal pardon restored the six men to their loved ones, but not before they had endured years of brutal exile. Their alleged crime? Seeking a living wage from their employers, they had formed a trade union in their quiet country village of Tolpuddle. It was not Britain's first union, as is sometimes reported, and was perfectly legal, but they were prosecuted under a different law relating to a mutinous navy, an absurd ruse which succeeded in a hostile court.

Today the six ordinary working men are revered throughout the trade union world as the Tolpuddle Martyrs. Their story is a hallowed chapter in the movement's history and known throughout the world, but what happened to them after their return from Australia is less well known. One stayed in Dorset, but the others joined the migrant flood across the Atlantic and found a new life for themselves and their wives and children in Canada…

English agriculture had boomed in the eighteenth century and the early years of the nineteenth, but slumped when the wars with France and the pressing need for home food production came to an end, leaving the landowners and large farmers richer than ever before and their poorly-paid employees facing poverty as jobs and wages were cut. The men's degradation was compounded by paltry parish relief and in some places by enclosure legislation which, while adding 6 million acres to the large estates, deprived many ordinary country-folk of their ancient rights to rear a domestic beast and grow food for their families on common land. In August 1830, the farm workers reacted with anger. The so-called Swing Riots erupted in south-east England, echoing the industrial unrest in other parts of the country, and spread westward, leaving a trail of burning crops. Threshing machines were damaged as symbols of modern farming techniques that were replacing the labour-intensive flail and taking away the mens' jobs.

Late in November the violence reached Dorset which had hitherto been regarded as a passive county, but the local gentry, uncomfortably aware of the general industrial and political unrest troubling the nation, feared that the infection of revolution had crossed the English Channel from France and hundreds of special constables were enrolled to help maintain order. The part-time soldiers of the Dorset Yeomanry, many of them farmers, were called in under the command of their colonel, James Frampton, a wealthy landowner in his sixties, Justice of the Peace (magistrate) and employer who pursued the unhappy farm workers with relentless determination. By the following year, fifty-five men had been arrested in Dorset and six sentenced to transportation to Australia, which had replaced North America as Britain's convict colony. Although the violence withered, the discontent over the dismal pay and conditions continued to flourish in the countryside. About four miles from Frampton's estate, the small thatched village of Tolpuddle began to stir from its rural slumber almost for the first time since the Romano-British rulers were taken over by the Saxons, who later succumbed to the Danes. The village lies in a picturesque fold of Dorset which the Danish/Saxon King Canute, who died in the county in 1035, had granted to Orc, his chief steward. Orc prefixed the name of the village, then known as Pindele, with that of his wife Tola, and Tolpiddle emerged, but centuries of indifferent spelling - or perhaps Victorian sensibilities - changed the 'I' to a 'u'. The 'i' remains defiant, however, in the nearby villages of Piddlehinton and Piddletrenthide, and the lush meadows along the river continue to be watered by the Piddle.

Regarded as the brightest of the Tolpuddle working men was a lay-preacher in the village's Wesleyan Methodist community. George Loveless had gathered a few publications, and while resting from long hours of toil in the fields, he taught himself to read and write by candlelight in the small thatched cottage he occupied with his wife, Elizabeth, and their three young children. An honest, upright man, he led a cap-in-hand deputation to the employers seeking a sorely-needed wage rise from 7s a week and pointing out that 10s was the rate being paid elsewhere. The men were given a promise of 9s, but it was never kept, and the wage slipped back to 7s with the threat of a starvation 6s. Meanwhile, food prices continued to rise until a loaf of bread cost about a shilling - or more than half a week's pay. Loveless appealed to the local magistrates in the innocent belief that they had the power to arbitrate over wages, only to be told that Parliament had expunged this right in 1824. Some Dorset clergy had warned then of labourers' families living almost entirely on potatoes and of one family of eleven sleeping in one room, but the Anglican vicar of Tolpuddle, the Reverend Thomas Warren, always denied that there had been an agreement at the farmers' meeting, which he had chaired. He was also a magistrate, and Loveless may not have been aware that behind the scenes the county magistrates were coming under increasing pressure from the Whig government to resist any concessions to wage-earners. During the 1830 riots, the Home Secretary and later Prime Minister, Lord Melbourne, had written to the Lord Lieutenant of Dorset, Lord Digby, regretting that Justices of the Peace in some parts of the country had supported a uniform rate of wages and the discontinuance of threshing machines. Further compliance could lead only to the most disastrous results, the letter warned, while giving the assurance that 'his majesty's government feels for the sufferings and privations which have of late years pressed and still continue to press severely upon the labouring classes'. The letter added that the government 'was anxious to adopt as speedily as possible every practicable and reasonable measure for their alleviation'. The minister's assurances must have sounded a little hollow to his critics.

Three years after the riots were suppressed, Loveless did not notice much 'alleviation' in Tolpuddle. He had read Robert Owen's pamphlet about the Cooperative Movement which advocated the formation of trade unions, and he knew that up and down the country Melbourne's 'labouring classes', as the minister called them, were combining to try and improve their wretched conditions. Loveless may also have been influenced by his brother John, who worked in the rope and net industry at the nearby town of Bridport and belonged to a union. Rebuffed by the magistrates, George decided to call a meeting of fellow farm workers. Denied access to a hall, they met under a sycamore tree on the village green in October 1833, and with the support of two union delegates from London, it was agreed to form the Friendly Society of Agricultural Labourers. Forty members joined, paying 1d a week subscription and a joining fee of 1s. The stage was set for a confrontation with the employers.

Unknown to the new union, two of the recruits were spies acting for squire Frampton, who employed one or both of them, and they told him that new members swore an oath of allegiance. Frampton mentioned this 'infamous pledge' in his frequent letters to the Home Secretary. Melbourne acknowledged that unions had been legalised in 1824, but he cunningly pointed out the existence of a law against the taking of unlawful oaths which Parliament had passed twenty-six years before. This legislation had been designed to quell a mutinous navy and was a ridiculous comparison, but Frampton took the hint and seized on it as a weapon to crush the 'mutineers' on his doorstep.

On 22 February 1834 posters went up in Tolpuddle warning that the taking of unlawful oaths could lead to seven years' transportation. Loveless must surely have noted that Frampton and his son Henry were among the nine magistrates named on the caution, so he could not have been entirely taken aback when two days later the village constable startled the early morning chill with a knock on his door. Loveless was arrested, along with his youngest brother James, brother-in-law James Brine, and three other 'mischievous and designing persons', as the poster put it: Thomas Standfield (also a Methodist lay-preacher), his son John Standfield, who was the only bachelor, and a sixth 'mutineer', James Hammett, who was the one non-Methodist. They scarcely had time to kiss their loved ones goodbye before being escorted by the constable on the seven mile trudge to the county jail in Dorchester where they were stripped, shorn, manacled, and locked in a damp, unheated, badly-lit cell for several weeks, sleeping on straw laid on the cold stone floor.

The trial opened on 17 March with the swearing-in of twelve jurors chosen for what should have been impartiality; but actually most of them were tenant farmers dependent on the estate owners for their livelihoods. The prosecution made much of the new society's initiation rites, which would undoubtedly sound strange in a union today. According to flimsy evidence given to the court on behalf of the prosecution, new members were obliged to swear loyalty to the union while kneeling blindfolded, and when the bandage was removed they were confronted by a 6ft high painting showing the skeleton of Death holding a scythe. Whereupon James Loveless, clad in a white surplice like his elder brother George, was said to have intoned 'Remember thine end,' and the new recruit kissed the Bible. The court seems not to have been told that other legitimate organisations employed an initiation vow without hindrance, including the Union of Flax Workers, and that was possibly significant, bearing in mind that George Loveless's brother John was a UFW member. A similar oath of unity and brotherhood was adopted by Canada's first lodge of the Oddfellows Friendly Society, formed in Montreal in the 1830s.

The two defence lawyers argued the legality of the Tolpuddle society and its 'wicked' loyalty pledge, and then Judge John Williams asked the defendants if they had anything to say. George Loveless passed him a note on which he had written:

> My Lord, if we have violated any law it was not done intentionally. We have injured no man's reputation, character, person, or property. We were uniting together to preserve ourselves, our wives and our children, from utter degradation and starvation. We challenge any man or number of men to prove that we have acted or intended to act different from the above statement.

The judge read out this noble plea, but mumbled the words and the jurors could not have heard them properly, but that did not matter for within twenty minutes they delivered their unanimous verdict – 'Guilty'. Judge Williams had made it clear that he was determined to make an example of the six defendants, and two days later he pronounced the maximum sentence for their 'heinous felony' – transportation to Australia for seven years. It is worth remembering that His Honour had been transported for life some time before – from the House of Commons to the privileged comfort of the House of Lords.

As George Loveless hobbled from the court, he tossed a piece of paper to onlookers in the street. On it he had copied a poem in the dim light of the cells that movingly expressed the men's feelings:

> God is our guide! From field from wave
> From plough from anvil and from loom
> We come our country's rights to save
> And speak a tyrant faction's doom;
> We raise the watchword 'Liberty' –
> We will, we will, we will be free!

'We WILL Be Free!'

God is our guide! No swords we draw,
We kindle not war's battle fires
By reason, union, justice, law,
We claim the birthright of our sires;
We raise the watchword 'Liberty' –
We will, we will, we **will** be free!

Loveless was said to be ill and was not with the other five while they waited in chains at Portsmouth for the prison ship that would take them to Australia. They were confined in the cramped, insanitary and rat-ridden lower deck of a floating hulk that was being used because the prisons on land were full. Punitive floggings were frequent and the victims soaked in salt water to heal the gaping wounds. Some weeks later the Tolpuddle five embarked on the four months' voyage to Botany Bay, New South Wales, where the treatment was no less brutal. They were forced to work on farms like slaves, without adequate food or beds or blankets, and the elder Standfield suffered severely from sores.

George Loveless was taken on a different ship to Tasmania (then known as Van Dieman's Land), and the delay fed the suspicion that his alleged illness had been used by Dorchester as a cunning device 'to separate the shepherd from his flock'. During two years working on the state governor's farm, he obviously impressed his employer and was given his liberty. The London newspapers were passed on to him, and from them he learned for the first time that the Tolpuddle men had been pardoned and granted a free passage home. He wrote immediately to his brother James, who spread the good news to the others in New South Wales; they had not been notified either.

The indignant demands for the men's release had continued, and within weeks of their conviction large crowds watched an estimated 50,000 protesters, including the representatives of nineteen trade unions, march down Whitehall to hand over a petition at the Home Secretary's office. Lord Melbourne refused to see them, but later the Whigs lost their majority in the House of Commons, and his Tory successor, Lord Russell, proved rather more sympathetic.

It was borne upon him that the offending oath was no more bizarre than the one sworn by the Orangemen, a secret society which included members of the royal family. But even after William IV grudgingly signed the pardon, the authorities procrastinated, and it was June 1837, the year of Queen Victoria's accession to the throne, before George Loveless finally stepped foot in England having spent more than three years abroad. His brother James, the Standfields and Brine followed three months later, but Hammett was not traced to a remote sheep-farm for some months, and when finally reunited with his wife and six-year-old son in August 1838, he had served more than four of his seven years' sentence. Yet his arrest had been a mistake. The warrant had actually named his younger brother John, but Hammett feared that a previous conviction for theft would count against his sibling at the trial and bravely kept the truth to himself. He was a martyr twice over.

The Tolpuddle men were warmly welcomed home by the Central Dorchester Committee, a London body of sympathisers who had supported the Dorset families from voluntary contributions, the magistrates having ordered that the wives and children should be denied parish aid. The committee had enough left in the kitty to buy the leases and equipment on two farms in Essex, each with two dwellings. The Loveless and Brine families moved into one farm and the Standfields and Hammetts occupied the other. After two years Hammett, ever the odd man out, returned to Tolpuddle with his wife and three children and laboured in the building trade for the rest of his working life.

Although George Loveless was now a successful farmer and man of property in Essex, he maintained his trade union beliefs and discussed them and his Methodism with local farm workers, an activity that annoyed an Anglican priest in the area who publicly denounced the newcomers as convicts and Nonconformist dissenters, and he complained to his superiors. Religious antagonism against Nonconformists is noted in the pamphlet *Victims of Whiggery* that Loveless wrote after his return from Australia, and, along with the prevailing national interest in their story, was a prime reason why, as the seven-year farm leases drew to their end in 1845, the Tolpuddle families decided to emigrate to Canada.

The transatlantic crossing to New York was marred by the untimely death of Sina Loveless, aged four, the younger of two daughters born to George and Elizabeth since his return from exile. The grieving families pressed on with their journey north by train and ferry to Ontario, then known as Upper Canada, and thence by ox-cart to the small town of London where they realised, perhaps for the first time, that their refuge from social strife had serious problems of its own. The presence of several hundred soldiers in the town was grim evidence of the climate of unrest lingering in Ontario after the suppression of the bloody Mackenzie Rebellion. Wisely the newcomers attached themselves to the staunchly Methodist community which steered a neutral course in the political dispute between the right-wing legislature and the radical reformists who wanted a US style of government, and they wisely bent their backs to till the Canadian soil, the task that had brought them many thousands of miles from their homeland. Undeterred by the troubles, George Loveless bought 100 acres of farmland at Bryanston (the name must have reminded him of its namesake in Dorset), about twelve miles from London, with a £25 deposit and a mortgage of £125, and he and Brine built a long homestead large enough to accommodate both families.

In later years, Loveless moved closer to London with his wife Elizabeth (known in the family as Betsy) and built a house at Siloam. Elizabeth died there in 1868 at the age of sixty-eight, followed by her husband six years later when he was seventy-seven. They lie together at the Methodist church that George had helped to build; their gravestone is engraved 'These are they who came out of great tribulation and washed their robes and made their way in the blood of the Lamb.' Their sons George and Robert eventually became property owners in their own right.

Brine stayed with the Lovelesses at Bryanston until he and his family moved to Clinton, but grasshoppers destroyed his hard-won crops and he purchased a more congenial property at Blanshard, about twenty-five miles north of London. He became a popular figure in the neighbourhood and was much mourned when he

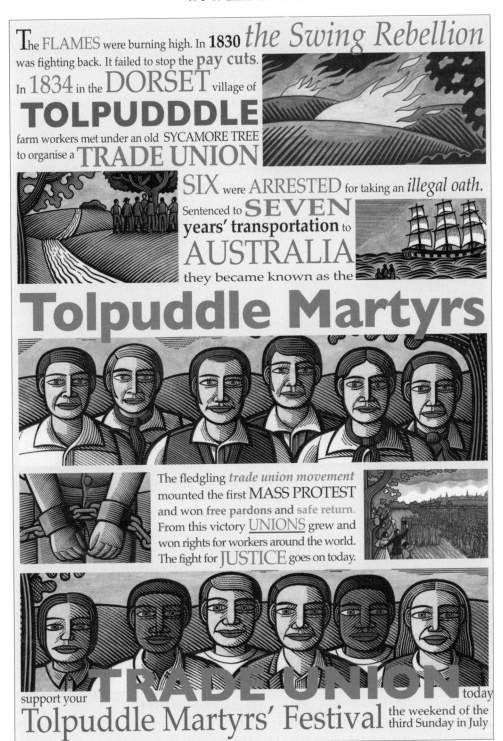

The FLAMES were burning high. In **1830** *the Swing Rebellion* was fighting back. It failed to stop the **pay cuts**. In **1834** in the **DORSET** village of **TOLPUDDLE** farm workers met under an old SYCAMORE TREE to organise a **TRADE UNION**

SIX were **ARRESTED** for taking an *illegal oath*. Sentenced to **SEVEN years' transportation** to **AUSTRALIA** they became known as the

Tolpuddle Martyrs

The fledgling *trade union movement* mounted the first MASS PROTEST and won **free pardons** and **safe return**. From this victory UNIONS grew and won rights for workers around the world. The fight for JUSTICE goes on today.

support your **TRADE UNION** today
Tolpuddle Martyrs' Festival the weekend of the third Sunday in July

Clifford Harper's story in pictures of the Tolpuddle Martyrs. (Reproduced by kind permission of the Trade Union Congress and the artist Clifford Harper) died in 1902 at the age of ninety. His wife Elizabeth, who had borne eleven children, was the same age when she passed away six years later. The younger Loveless, James, did not follow the way of the other Dorset men into farming; he took a post as sexton of a Methodist church in North Street, London, where he served until his retirement. After the death of his wife, Sarah, he married again and fathered a third child. After his death in February 1873 at the age of sixty-five, he was buried in the Methodist cemetery in London; when the site was sold he was reinterred in Mount Pleasant cemetery.

The Standfields arrived a little after the Lovelesses and Brines. Thomas and his son John took over a plot not far from the others at Bryanston. Thomas died in 1864 at the age of seventy-four, and was followed a year later by his wife Diana, known within the family as Dinneah. Son John added four more children to the two he and Elizabeth had brought from Essex, and branched into commerce with two stores in Bryanston, and then ownership of a hotel in East London where he became a respected figure in local affairs and served for a time as Reeve, the Canadian equivalent of an English mayor. Possessed of his father's fine voice, he founded a Methodist choir that became well-known in Western Ontario. Relatives had followed from England, among them George's brother John, the unionist flax dresser. Nowadays, direct descendants of the Dorset families have spread both sides of the Canada/US border. Members of the Loveless and Standfield families lie in London's Siloam cemetery where, in 1959, the Prime Minister of Ontario unveiled a plaque in honour of the Martyrs, and ten years later the Labour Memorial Park was opened and dedicated to them.

The Martyrs have also been memorialised in Tolpuddle in the heart of Dorset. Seventy-eight years after they sailed from England, a distinguished member of the British Parliament and Chairman of the Labour Party, Arthur Henderson, unveiled a memorial arch over the gateway to the Methodist Chapel that replaced the old one where the Martyrs prayed. A lifelong Methodist, Henderson went on to high government office and was awarded the Nobel Peace Prize in 1934 for presiding over the Geneva disarmament conference. The simple arch bears the inscription, 'Erected in honour of the faithful and brave men of this village who in 1834 suffered transportation in the cause of liberty, justice and righteousness, which is a stimulus to our own and future generations.' The ruin of the old chapel is next door to Standfield's thatched cottage now marked by a blue plaque where, in a room upstairs, the Martyrs took the oath that led to their misfortune.

Those 'faithful and brave men' have inspired the national Trades Union Congress (TUC) to pay homage to them in many other ways over the years. Every July hundreds of Labour and union supporters, including members of the government, parade through the village to the green where the Martyrs made trade union history.

The tree believed to be the original sycamore had decayed and had to be felled, and in 1984 Lionel Murray, the then TUC General Secretary, planted a seedling from it with a commemorative plaque. But was the ivy-covered stump that remains the original tree which visitors come from many parts of the world to see? Doubts were

Tombstone of George Loveless, Edmonton, Alberta. (The Dorset Natural History & Archaeological Society, The Dorset County Museum)

raised in 2005 when forestry experts dated another sycamore flourishing on the site as being 320 years old – in other words, it was old and large enough to have been the original tree that sheltered the Martyrs' historic meeting. Who knows?

The Dorchester court was opened as a memorial to the Martyrs in 1956, looking exactly as it did in 1834, with the simple wooden stalls where they pleaded their lost cause before an unheeding jury, and the Royal Arms of William III over the seat from which Judge Williams delivered his fateful verdict. Preserved under the court is the infamous cell in which the Martyrs were held during their trial. To mark the centenary of the trial, the TUC opened a row of six cottages and a meeting hall in Tolpuddle for retired farm workers; each cottage bears the name of one of the Martyrs.

The only monument to James Hammett, who stayed in Dorset when the other five Martyrs left England for good, is a simple headstone that the TUC erected on his grave which is otherwise unmarked in the shadow of trees in the churchyard of St John the Evangelist. Three times married and the father of six children, he never enjoyed the prosperity of his fellow martyrs, and when he died in a Dorchester home for the elderly at the age of eighty, he was almost blind and largely forgotten.

In the motor age the little village grew busy with vehicles heading for Dorchester and the west, but now it is peaceful following the construction of a bypass. The petrol station, shop and Post Office have gone, but the farm workers cottages and that famous village green still remain. Off the main road a narrow country lane lined with thick hedges winds down from the green towards the river between pastures and ploughed fields. Along this quiet road the Martyrs will have plodded wearily up to their humble homes and impoverished families after toiling long hours on their employer's estate. The present must have looked bleak then; they could never have imagined that a bright future awaited them thousands of miles away in the New World.

In the year 2000 the TUC gave a £20,000 commission to a noted sculptor, Thompson Dagnall, and a year later the gleaming white monument was erected on the grass sward in front of the retirees' cottages, which now include a museum. Hewn in sandstone from the Purbeck Hills that roll along the horizon on the opposite side of the river valley, six small columns represent 'the faithful and brave men of this village'. Before them a life-size figure of their leader, George Loveless, barefoot in his old farm workers' smock, looks upwards as if proclaiming to the heavens 'We will, we will, we **will** be free!', as indeed – in Canada – they were.

12

The Making of British Columbia

The Canadian Far West, between the Pacific Ocean and the snow-capped Rocky Mountains, was a largely untroubled wilderness until the discovery of gold brought 30,000 prospectors swarming into the Fraser Valley to dig and pan for their dreams along the river banks. As most of them were American, Britain feared a takeover by its Republican neighbour to the south and hurriedly sent a unit of Royal Engineers in 1858 to reinforce its sovereignty and prepare this huge piece of empire for development. The army specialists marked out a clear border with the USA, surveyed and mapped, hacked and blasted hundreds of miles of roads and tracks through forests and mountains, flung bridges across river torrents, cleared settlement sites, and planned the future capital. Through their skills and military presence the Royal Engineers, or 'sappers' as they are known, enabled the confirmation of British rule and averted a confrontation with the States – yet they never numbered more than 200. Disbanded after five years, nearly all except the officers settled with their families in the territory they had opened up. Their commander returned to Britain for further duties before retiring to Dorset where he lived his remaining twenty years so inconspicuously that his empire-building career is little known in the county. But an ocean and a continent away, Major-General Richard Clement Moody is venerated in British Columbia as a co-founder of Canada's third largest and most spectacular province.

He was born to the military life on 13 February 1813. His first sight of the world was a garrison in Barbados, and when old enough he followed his father, Thomas, and elder brother, Hampden, into the British Army's specialist corps, the Royal Engineers. Like them he rose to the rank of Colonel. Another brother, the Reverend J.L. Moody, became an army chaplain. Richard trained at the Royal Military Academy in London, saw active service in Ireland and the West Indies, and then returned to the Academy as Professor of Fortification. At the age of twenty-eight he was appointed the first governor of the Falklands since the eviction of the Argentine occupiers and the British repossession of the islands. 'The colony was almost in a state of anarchy,' according to an official report 'and the young governor was given exceptional powers which he used with great wisdom and moderation during his term of office.' After nearly nine years in the lonely South Atlantic, he brought back to Britain a native variety of grass, the tall-growing tussock, which won him a Royal Agricultural Society gold award for his enterprise. Gold, of a different kind, was to figure rewardingly in his future career.

He was commanding the sappers in the north of England in 1852 when the Holmfirth Reservoir in Yorkshire burst its banks with considerable loss of life and damage to property, and he produced a report on the disaster and the condition of other large reservoirs in the region. In that same year the thirty-nine-year-old officer married Mary Susannah Hawks, daughter of the Deputy Lieutenant (Queen's representative) in Newcastle on Tyne, where he was based. After a brief spell as Governor of Malta and promotion to Colonel, he took charge of the sappers in the whole of northern Britain, including Scotland where, as a skilled architect, he drew up the restoration plans for Edinburgh Castle and showed them to Queen Victoria.

The greatest challenge of his career awaited him in the westernmost province of Canada. For some years the vast mainland, four times the size of Britain, had been run on behalf of the government by the Hudson's Bay Company from its base on the offshore colony of Vancouver Island, but in 1858 the lucrative fur trade with the indigenous Indians was rudely thrown into turmoil when the Fraser gold rush erupted, bringing shiploads of rowdy prospectors scrambling to the mainland from the petering minefields of California and elsewhere in the United States. Amid old fears of American expansionism, the fur company's chief representative on Vancouver, James Douglas, donned his other hat as the island colony's governor and extended his authority to the mainland, then known as New Caledonia. The Imperial government, realising that gold was overtaking furs as the principal cash crop, quickly approved his initiative and raised New Caledonia to full colonial status as British Columbia. Douglas gave up his position with Hudson's Bay on appointment as fulltime governor of both the island colony and the new one, with the assistance of a judge, Matthew Begbie, and a police commissioner to enforce British law and order. The choice of deputy governor in charge of land and works fell on a colonel who had himself governed two colonies and was now commander of the Royal Engineers being hurried from England to develop British Columbia.

Moody reached Vancouver on Christmas Day 1858 with his wife and four children and a party of sappers. Within two or three weeks he was thrust into the raw reality of his latest challenge. An American was reported to be inciting anti-British feelings in one of the mining villages spreading along the Fraser Valley, and on a wintry January day, Moody set out with an armed party of twenty-two of his sappers and some marines and seamen from the Royal Navy, to escort Judge Begbie and a constable to deal with the disturbance. The steamer carrying his force got stuck on midstream ice in the Fraser River, but a small detachment reached the camp on foot and canoe and, undeterred by warning bullets fired over their heads, arrested the troublemaker. At the trial in a makeshift court crammed with tough miners, Moody and the judge were the only ones present without a gun. The offender must have been so impressed with this evidence of British justice that after paying a fine for his disorderly conduct, he offered to conduct the judge on a tour of the diggings, and after it Moody joined them to share a bottle of champagne.

'Ludicrous as the incident may seem,' writes Beth Hill in her book *Sappers, the Royal Engineers in British Columbia,* 'this comic opera war set the pattern for a well-regulated and non-violent gold rush and the peaceful development of the new colony.' Thereafter, she concludes, the Fraser goldfields experienced none of the lawlessness that characterised those of California and, later on, Alaska, but there were isolated incidents of friction caused by miners intruding on the Indians' traditional hunting and ceremonial grounds. Following one fatal outbreak of violence, Governor Douglas met the Indian chiefs, and the calming presence of thirty-five sappers allayed the full scale Indian war he dreaded. But the disputes over land rights still rankle.

Back on the steamboat after the January drama, Moody collapsed from the bitter cold and discomfort, but soon recovered and rejoined his family in crowded Victoria, the capital of the Vancouver colony. The boatloads of US miners heading for the Fraser, and the numerous enterprises that sprang up to serve them, had swollen the population of the small town from several hundred to over 5,000 almost overnight. He complained of having 'no Office, no Clerks, a very tiny house full of my dear children, but whose shouts sometimes "fun", sometimes "wailing", do not tend to compose the thoughts.' Mary was not happy either, but as the weather improved, the family moved to a spacious official residence on the mainland built by the sappers and hired labour.

The site was destined to be the capital of British Columbia and grandly called New Westminster, but in the beginning it was not much more than a forest clearing with huts and tents, surrounded by the fallen trunks of huge trees. Later in 1859, Moody heard the sad news that his brother Hampden, commanding the Royal Engineers in Northern Ireland, had died in Belfast.

While the road and trail construction went on apace, despite the vicious mosquitoes, Moody and his sappers were thrust into yet another ominous situation. A party of 460 US soldiers landed on San Juan, one of a cluster of islands close to the Vancouver colony and occupied by both Britons and Americans. Moody led a small force of fifteen sappers to San Juan, and they went ashore under cover of Royal Navy guns. The atmosphere between the opposing sides was tense, but reason prevailed, and it was agreed that the island should be run jointly until the sovereignty was settled, which it was - twelve years later. The confrontation had the effect of extending the sappers' stay in British Columbia. There had been talk of returning them to Britain on the grounds of expense, but they had demonstrated their worth and soldiered on for a further three years.

Behind the San Juan dispute was the chequered history of Oregon, south of British Columbia. Both countries claimed it and the islands off the coast, but thousands of land-hungry settlers had settled there, following the United States' urging to 'Go West' along the 2,000 mile Oregon Trail from the Mid-West with their covered wagons, horses and cattle, and they overwhelmed Britain's claim. Ownership was formally conceded in a treaty signed in 1846, under which the US, for its part, recognised Vancouver Island as indisputably British, even though it remained obstinately below the 49th parallel of latitude which Washington DC and Ottawa had agreed should constitute their mutual frontier right across the continent, from the Great Lakes in the east to the Pacific coast. After some years the frontier was 'bent' on the map to go round and away from the island.

On the mainland the Fraser gold rush made the delineation of British Columbia's southern border with Oregon (part of which is now Washington State) a political priority. The sappers traced the 49th parallel with their surveying instruments and telescopes and, with hired help and the participation of the American boundary team, a corridor or vista hundreds of miles long was cleared through thick forests and over two mountain ranges, and iron markers were planted at intervals to indicate the border. It was a remarkable achievement.

Moody lyricised in a letter to England about the scenic views from the mouth of the Fraser River:

> Extending miles to the right and left are low marsh lands, and yet there is a background of superb mountains, Swiss in outline, dark in woods and grandly towering into the clouds. There is a sublimity that impresses you. Everything is large and magnificent, worthy of the entrance to the Queen of England's dominions on the Pacific mainland.

As a practical soldier, however, Moody judged that the chosen site for Her Majesty's new colony was vulnerable, with the US only twenty miles away. 'At any moment the Americans could and would have their grip on the very throat of British Columbia,' he warned and switched the capital from the southern to the northern bank of the Fraser so that an enemy would have to ford the river. The switch reflected the lingering suspicion of US ambitions, although the prospect of becoming one of the stars on the Republican flag was not entirely unattractive to some in the British colony.

The sappers were into their fourth year and the Fraser gold fever was dying down when new strikes were reported further north. The miners grabbed their sieves and shovels and headed for the Caribou Mountains, where they were joined by pioneers from Eastern Canada, the British Isles and Europe who crossed the Canadian prairies and the Rocky Mountains over a trail that was just as arduous and heroic as the Oregon Trail, but has been less romanticised.

Impressed by the increasing revenue from the issue of mining licences and the sales of land, Governor Douglas could see the financial benefit of making the Caribou goldfields more accessible, and Moody sent his men to plan a 400 mile route for a new road into the interior. They constructed the first and most hazardous section themselves, dynamiting through solid rock, and at one stage they worked on the steep side of a narrow canyon looking down on the Fraser River raging 800ft below. Contractors took on the rest of the sappers' plans for the road until snow ended construction for the winter. The Caribou Road is applauded today as a feat of engineering to match the building of the trans-Canada railway across the Rockies, and sections of it have been incorporated in the modern highway leading to the Caribou Mountains.

Mary Moody confided in a letter to her mother in May 1863 that her husband was looking very old and not quite well and needed a change. That change came only two months later when the Colonial Office ordered the end of the sappers' unit. All its members were granted land at a favourable price, and most chose to settle in the colony. The officers, with one exception, embarked for Britain and sailed amid the affectionate cheers of a crowd on the quay and the strains of *Auld Lang Syne* played by the sappers' band. The parting is recalled by a painting hanging in New Westminster's City Hall, which shows Douglas and Begbie bidding Moody farewell. 'When all was over and the bustle and excitement consequent upon leave-taking had subsided,' reported the *British Columbian* newspaper, 'a feeling of sadness and gloom seemed to pervade the entire community.'

General Richard Clement Moody. (The Royal Engineers Museum and Library)

Moody, now squire of 3,750 acres of British Columbia which cost him an average $2 per acre to buy, took over the Royal Engineers in Chatham district close to the London area for two years, and then, after promotion to Major-General in January 1886, he retired on full pay to Dorset, where he took up residence with Mary and their nine children in the small harbour town of Lyme Regis. He seems to have taken little or no part in local affairs, except for a period when the skills that had led the military contribution to the creation of a huge Canadian province presided over a commission to review the tranquil Dorset border with the adjoining county of Somerset.

At the age of seventy-four, he was staying in Bournemouth fifty miles along the coast from Lyme Regis when on 31 March 1887 he died from apoplexy in the resort's prestigious Royal Bath Hotel. Canadians occasionally pay homage to his modest grave at St Peter's parish church, but until it was vandalised in December 1988, Bournemouth residents were generally unaware of the empire-builder laid to rest in their midst. A local stonemason carried out repairs free of charge and a British Columbian residing in Bournemouth obtained a maintenance grant from his home government to ensure that Moody's last resting place would be properly looked after, but it continues to be overshadowed in public interest by the tombs of better-known celebrities, notably Mary Shelley, the author of *Frankenstein* and wife of the poet Percy Bysshe Shelley, whose heart is said to be buried there.

Out in British Columbia, however, there is much to remind its citizens of the achievements of Moody and his talented sappers. They are credited with giving the mainland its first government printing office, newspaper, building society, social club, schoolhouse, Protestant church, and private hospital, and designing the province's first coat of arms and postage stamp. The first legislative assembly in British Columbia met in the barracks the sappers left behind them. New Westminster inherited from them its wide avenues, squares and parks, and Moody Park displays a plaque erected 'to honour Colonel Richard Clement Moody, R.E, who selected New Westminster to be the capital of the mainland colony of British Columbia'.

Behind the inscription's closing words echo the fact that the capital he planned was replaced after only two years by another new town, Vancouver, not far away, but here again there is evidence of the sappers' work. Moody set 1,000 acres aside for the city's spectacular recreation ground, Stanley Park, which is surrounded on three sides by the Pacific Ocean and overlooked by Grouse Mountain, nearly 4,000ft high. Within its perimeter are 1,000 trees, a zoo, and many sports facilities. 'The people of Vancouver owe their splendid park as well as the University Endowment Lands to the commanding officer of the Royal Engineers,' says Beth Hill.

The removal of the seat of government from New Westminster must have been sad news for Moody just a year before he died. Capital status ultimately crossed the narrow strait to Victoria on Vancouver Island. After these disruptions, New Westminster declined but is recovering and returning to Moody's vision of a fine city. British Columbia, much visited by UK tourists, is regarded as the most 'English' of the Canadian provinces, and Victoria was once described by Rudyard Kipling as a blend of Bournemouth and other English resorts, with a touch of Naples Bay and the Himalayas. Living up to its name, Victoria regards itself as 'the Royal City'.

But what of Moody the man? A glowing obituary was written of the Dorset resident by an army colleague, 'No man who knew him failed to love the kindly Christian gentleman whose seventy-four years of life were devoted to the service of God, his sovereign, and his neighbour.'

Murder and Suicide

Bournemouth has a link with British Columbia other than the grave of General Moody – a gruesome link. The architect of the province's Parliament building in Victoria was brutally murdered in the Dorset resort and afterwards his wife, a Canadian pianist and composer of popular songs, stabbed herself to death on the banks of a local river.

The tragic story of Francis Rattenbury and Alma Woolf is notorious in Britain and the subject of a recent television programme in British Columbia. The couple met in 1930 at one of the fine buildings he designed in Canada, the distinctive Gothic-style Empress Hotel, the most prestigious hotel in Victoria. He was there as the guest at a function and she was entertaining at the piano. They fell in love, and she moved into his house in Victoria, although he already had a wife living there with their two daughters, albeit in a separate wing. The ménage à trois did not suit Florrie Rattenbury, and she divorced him.

He was free to marry Alma, and in 1934 they set up home in Bournemouth and had a child, but his attempted return to his professional career was not very successful, while she blossomed, performing at concerts, broadcasting on the radio, recording, and publishing her own compositions. She had been married twice before but was younger than Rattenbury, who was in his sixties when into their lives came a handsome young man of nineteen, whom they employed as a live-in handyman. George Stoner became obsessed with this attractive woman who returned his affection, and in a fit of jealousy he bashed her husband over the head. He confessed to murder at the trial and was sentenced to be hanged, but the verdict was later commuted to life, and in three years he was released to join the wartime army. Alma was found not guilty of complicity in the murder, but the public reaction was hostile to her role in the affair, and she killed herself.

13

Schoolma'am Goes West

The proprietor of a thriving private school didn't particularly want to go to America with her two children, but her footloose husband did, and their early adventure in Texas is like an episode from a Wild West movie…

Alone in Texas, husband away, prim schoolmistress from Christchurch, England, makes desperate bid to flee enemies. Armed with gun, hitches up Victorian skirt, clambers on wagon, grabs reins, slaps horse into action. Swaying and bumping behind her, teenage sons point rifles back along dusty trail.

Signpost Cypress River ferry. Galloping pursuers take short cut. Reach Jefferson first. John Wayne-type sheriff questions riders. They swear she owes them money. He is shocked by their heartless chase of a mother and children. Orders men out of town at point of his guns.

Family arrive too late. Paddle steamer already streaming black smoke on way back to New Orleans. Dismayed family, stranded on a deserted quay, belongings around them.

Flashback. Sailing ship crowded with immigrants. Close up: buttoned up heroine Mary Ann Smith with wayward husband Henry, excited sons Thomas and Edward. New Orleans approaches…

All this is cinematic invention, of course, but close in essence to Mary Ann's real-life adventure in Texas which she relates, without celluloid melodrama, in her own account of their many fortunes and misfortunes in pioneer America. She wrote her diary in remarkable detail for a woman of eighty-four. Many years later the pages were yellowed and falling apart (some may even have been lost) when a relative[2] typed them out, but her delicate nineteenth-century handwriting enabled him to decipher much of what she describes as her 'chequered life' on both sides of the Atlantic.

She was born in London on 1 April 1808, which was a Friday, and by a 'singular coincidence', four generations of her family were born on the same day of the week - her paternal grandparents, her father and his brother, and her own sons. She had often laughed at the superstition that Friday was an unlucky day, but had pondered

2 Detmar A. Andersen, husband of great-granddaughter Gladys Winter Andersen. Her mother was the relative for whom Mary Ann wrote her memoirs.

over it because, she says, there was so much that could not be understood in the world of nature. When she was about eighteen months old, her parents, Thomas and Susannah (surname Barrow not mentioned in the transcript), moved from the capital to the small town of Christchurch on the south-west coast of England, where he took over the management of a company producing a small component for contemporary watches and clocks known as a fusee chain. Some examples were so fine they could be threaded through the eye of a needle, and they all demanded special skill and precision from her father, who was responsible for the making of the links, and from the women workers, who assembled them together with pin-size rivets. In and around Christchurch the industry employed hundreds of women and children; some in small factories or their own cottages, others in workhouses for the poor.

For many years the Christchurch fusee chain was exported to America and other parts of the world until superseded by the modern escapement mechanism later in the century. This almost forgotten industry is explored by the historian Allen White in his book *The Fusee Chainmakers*, recently republished by the Christchurch Local History Society, which also holds a copy of the transcript.

From the age of nine, Mary Ann attended the Sabbath or Sunday School run by a dynamic Congregationalist minister, the Reverend Daniel Gunn, who made a lasting impression on the religious life of Christchurch and on her, for she adhered to the dissenting church for the rest of her days. When 'a select boarding school for young ladies' opened in Christchurch, she became the first pupil and showed such exceptional aptitude in the kind of studies and handicrafts thought 'proper' for girls in those days that she was offered a partnership by a woman starting a rival establishment. Only fourteen then, Mary Ann recalls 'I was ambitious and thought it would be splendid to be independent, and I very foolishly promised her I would.' In her eagerness, she failed to consult her father who 'highly disapproved', suspecting exploitation of his young daughter, but he reluctantly gave his consent. His misgivings proved to be justified; for more than a year she was made to slave until late in the evenings, teaching pupils, correcting exercises and arranging needlework until, cheated of half the financial reward that was due to her, she obeyed her father's insistence and quit. In the event, she had learned a lot from her employer about running a girls' school, and urged by a number of the parents she opened her own with eighteen pupils – and she was still only fifteen years old. The experience was to serve her well in America, but also brought trouble.

Her father spent his evenings relaxing at home with his hobby, taxidermy, which was much favoured in those days, and the well-to-do would call wanting a favourite bird or animal preserved. According to her account, one aristocratic caller was Lord Cornwallis, a 'grey-headed blustering old gentlemen' who had surrendered his army to the Americans during the War of Independence and desired the preservation of the horse he had with him at Yorktown. Her father was too busy to undertake the commission, and Mary Ann never forgot how the general 'swore and raved' at the refusal.

At the age of twenty-two, while staying with a woman friend on the English Channel Island of Guernsey, she met Henry Smith who was 'the cause of changing the whole course' of her life. He had learned her secret, that she was heiress to a 'considerable property' in London. As she realised later, he was 'always on the lookout for a wife with money' and thought she was 'just the bait for his hook'. She resisted his blandishments, but he followed her to Christchurch with a marriage proposal which broke her engagement to another man. Two years later she and Henry were married. Only two days into their honeymoon on the Isle of Wight in Christchurch Bay, he revealed his 'true motive' for the marriage. He asked his bride about her inheritance and was taken aback to hear that she had been cheated out of it by a relative with a forged will. 'His remarks showed me what I had to look forward to (and) had I then disclosed to my parents what he said I might have saved myself years of misery'.

Cholera broke out while they were living in Guernsey, and on doctor's advice she sailed for Christchurch to have her first child. Thomas was three months old when she finally ventured back to the Channel Islands and Jersey where her husband had moved, with as many of their belongings as had not been stolen in Guernsey or burned because of the infection. Undaunted, and by now a practised businesswoman, she opened what she calls 'a fancy shop' and taught ornamental needlework and drawing.

When the principal of a young ladies' seminary died in Guernsey, Mary Ann took it over and ran it 'with satisfaction and profit (for) three terms, but my husband was so unsettled and of such a roving disposition he soon tired of a place'. He wrote to her father, and as a result they left the island and worked in the Christchurch business. Henry travelled with watch-making samples, and often she did not see or hear from him for periods of eight or nine months. Meanwhile, she was running her own school in the town.

When the transatlantic tide of European migrants became a flood, she could not have been surprised that Henry was eager to seek a new life in America, but he lacked the financial means, having spent all he ever earned and had never provided for the family. He urged her to raise the necessary money on some valuable specimens of stuffed birds her father had given her and promised that if she would go with him to America, he would devote the rest of his life to making her happy. 'What woman, who had for so many years been hungering for the love of her husband, would have refused?' she asks. An unworthy husband might receive a different answer from a modern wife, but this was the nineteenth century, and Mary Ann conceded. With a collateral loan on the valuable taxidermy gifts from her father, she bought some acres of Texas advertised by a land company and six tickets for the voyage. The news that two of the tickets were for her beloved parents so horrified a baronet friend of her father he travelled as fast as four horses could cover fifty miles and pleaded with him not to let his 'crazy daughter…drag him off to America'. Thomas Barrow, now in his mid-fifties, was paralysed down one side of his body, and the friend feared that even if he survived the journey he would not be able to endure the hardships and climate of the country which he, the friend, had seen. She was heartbroken at the realisation that her beloved parents would not accompany the family to America, but Henry promised they would return to Christchurch within five years. In fact, she would never again see the quaint little town with a centuries-old church the size of a cathedral and a crumbling castle watching over the harbour and out to sea…

On the first day of May 1848, the family sailed from Liverpool bound for their promised home in Texas. Just two months had passed since the end of the US war with Spanish-speaking Mexico that won the Lone Star state its independence, and no doubt Mary Ann was wondering what her family would find in this strange new land as they stepped ashore in Louisiana after nine weeks on the Atlantic. They had planned to continue by riverboat to Shreveport in the north of the state and thence by wagon across the Texas border to Dallas County, but a bitter shock was waiting for them in New Orleans. Mary Ann was bluntly told by the land company agent that under the sales agreement she had arrived too late to take possession of the land she thought was hers and had lost it, along with the money she had paid. She felt swindled and feared for her loved ones adrift in a strange country. Where would they go? Henry took a pragmatic view – they had come from Christchurch with the intention of going to Texas and to Texas they would go, come what may. As if to compound their misery, a violent storm broke while their baggage was being transferred to the ferry boat, and the loaders worked knee-deep in water.

On dry land at Shreveport, Mary Ann bought provisions for the onward wagon trek without knowing what they would do in Texas when they got there and where they would live. The store assistant, an Englishman, recognised that she was a schoolma'am, and before handing over her purchases he went outside without saying a word. He returned with six men who wanted to talk to her, and she feared she was about to be robbed yet again.

To her relief they explained that they understood she was a teacher and wondered if she would take the position left vacant at the local school by the death of the incumbent. They offered Mary Ann $1,000 a year if she would take the job, and Henry, a skilled carpenter, could have all the contracts for building that he chose to take. At the hotel where the family had booked rooms, she learned that Shreveport was so unhealthy no resident unused to the climate would live for long, and three teachers had died there within a few months. The teaching offer was politely declined.

There was another option. Two fellow passengers on the steamer, an English couple returning to the Texan town of Daingerfield, had heard of the family's dilemma and said they could stay in their home while looking around for somewhere to live. Mary Ann and Henry accepted their kindness with gratitude and departed from Shreveport on a covered wagon heading for Daingerfield (spelt without the first 'i' in the transcript). After three or four miles the drivers stopped in a wood, and the family camped in the wagon, a 'novel way to spend the night', she observes, but the nocturnal noise of birds, frogs and insects and the thunder and vivid lightning of a drenching storm kept them awake:

> I had not a dry stitch of clothing and could get at nothing to change (into) as everything was packed and my clothes had to dry on my back. You (*her granddaughter for whom the account was written*) will not be surprised when I tell you that in two days I was taken down with fever and ague (*malarial fever*) and continued sick all of our hundred (*actually eighty-two*) mile journey, and the roads were nothing but sloughs and holes. We were no sooner prised out of one than

we were in another, frequently not going five miles a day, and I remained sick nearly a month after we reached our friends at Daingerfield, but the neighbours were extremely kind, coming to care for me by day and sending a faithful negress[3] to watch me through the night. At first all thought I could not live, but at last an English doctor named Freeman was called, and after about a week's attendance I began to mend.

With what money was left after meeting the doctor's bills, she entered into an agreement to purchase by instalments five acres of land containing a house on the edge of Daingerfield. The house, like most of those in the town, was built of logs, for Daingerfield still had the atmosphere of a pioneer settlement about it; only three years had passed since the end of the US–Mexico war gave Texas (a territory as big as France) admission to the Union as the 28th state. Henry made additions to the Smiths' house, and when word got around that they were of wood-frame construction, he built several wood-frame houses in the town.

As at Shreveport Mary Ann was soon being begged to return to the blackboard and despite feeling weak from her illness, she consented and reopened the nearby schoolhouse with forty pupils. A dormitory extension was added to accommodate the eleven boarders and a staff engaged consisting of the daughter of a prominent planter as an assistant teacher and two hired black women. By the end of term Mary Ann had earned enough to make the first payment on her property.

The parents were kind to her and often sent a horse for her to ride in company with their children when, once a month, the boarders went home for the weekend. Her sons were befriended by local families and enjoyed hunting and fishing with them. Henry made the acquaintance of one or two English families living a mile or two out of town, raising her hopes that he would settle down for a few years. There was a less welcome side to their situation.

> I could not say that I ever liked the people of the town, they were so rough. There were two saloons in sight of the schoolhouse, and it was no uncommon sight to witness a drunken fight and see a man ride by with blood pouring from a wound where he had been stabbed or another with his eye gouged out. The climate was very trying to me, there was much malarial fever, and I was not infrequently obliged by poor health to close my school for a week to gain strength.

In 1849 reports of gold discoveries in the Sacramento Valley excited a rush of Daingerfield men to California and stimulated Henry's old urge to be on the move, albeit in the opposite direction. He mentioned Mobile in Alabama where, he said, the wages were higher for a good mechanic and the climate was more amenable, but she refused to approve. 'I did not feel like being left there with only the two boys in such a community to fight life's battle alone.' It seems that the school board was proposing to open a women's seminary, a larger school with her in charge,

---

3 Use of this description is a reminder that Texas was a slave state until the end of the Civil War in 1865.

and he would get the building contract if he gave the board $50. Quite why the members expected the money is not entirely clear from the diary, but she maintains that he never intended to pay it until she commenced another five-month term, and 'he led them on by indecision'. He promised to return home from Mobile after five months and would send her money meanwhile, but she never received any and finally resolved to join him. She tried to collect outstanding school fees, but some parents refused to pay; she describes them as 'border roughs' who had fled from other states for various crimes, including murder. One threatened to shoot her husband if he asked for the fee, and the board continued to press for the $50. She felt 'harassed and perplexed' and almost desperate, but 'stoutly' refused the board's demand, alleging that Henry's name on a document was a forgery. Was this the absolute truth or a wifely defence of a spouse? We shall never know.

Mary Ann gathered what payments she could, paid her debts, sold their home, and hired two wagons, one self-drive and the other with a driver, to transport the family and their belongings to the steamer port on the Cypress River. What actually happened on the day of her getaway dash from Daingerfield is just as fascinating and eventful as the fiction that opened this chapter, and is no different in essence.

That very morning, the six members of the school board 'marched to the house' and threatened that unless the $50 were paid she would not be allowed to leave town and her goods would be seized. 'Gentlemen,' she replied, 'I am going to leave this afternoon, and if anyone dares to try to stop me he will be shot, for my two sons, the driver, and myself will all have firearms back and front of the two wagons and will certainly use them.' They walked off, but although she fully expected trouble driving out of town they did not come near her again. 'I suppose they were ashamed to treat a woman so, but they went on to the next town about 30 miles away called Jefferson to get the sheriff to stop us there. This I found out afterwards.' The family reached Jefferson fifteen minutes too late; the last ferry of the season had just left. 'I was thoroughly discouraged, my luggage was all unloaded at the wharf, and I knew no-one there. The boys were amusing themselves shooting at alligators, of which the bayou [river marsh] was full.'

She was sitting on a wooden chest and pondering where the family could stay when a kindly stranger got her luggage stored and offered the hospitality of his house if his wife could accommodate the family. He thought another steamer would come within a week, but none was seen. There was an anxious moment in his home one evening when a dinner guest sitting opposite Mary Ann asked if anyone had seen two wagons with a woman and two sons in town. She anxiously wagged a finger to warn the host not to let on, and he gallantly denied having seen them. The guest related that the woman was the teacher from Daingerfield, and the school governors had tried 'infamously' to extort money from her for which they had no claim.

Mary Ann realised with relief that the speaker was the town sheriff as he explained that he had been asked to stop the teacher and attach her goods, but he told them he would 'disable the right arm of any man' who attempted to molest her. Mary Ann rose from the table, revealed that she was the woman, and thanked the sheriff for protecting her and the boys. He shook her hand in 'real Southern fashion' and wished her God speed to her journey's end.

There was still no sign of a ferry after more than a week, and then an old German teamster agreed to take the family and their luggage on his wagon to catch the steamboat at Shreveport for New Orleans. His little boy riding alongside offered her the chance to ride on his pony for part of each day, the weather was fine, and she would have enjoyed the journey had it not been so 'tedious'. After a two-day wait for the ferry at Shreveport the family were at last on their way to New Orleans – but not to the end of their troubles. A day or so into the voyage the boys were taken sick with bilious fever, and she was giving them a glass of water at about 3 a.m. when she was suddenly thrown across the cabin. 'Then ensued a scene I shall never forget,' she writes. Passengers leapt out of their berths and rushed on deck. Women were screaming and jumping overboard on to the deck of the steamer that had caused the collision. They called on her to join them as the stricken boat was sinking. 'More than terrified', she asked the pilot if this were true because she had two sick boys in the cabin and all their belongings were in the hold. He replied that they were moving on to a sand bar and would return to deeper water when the damage was repaired. 'So I stayed with the boys, the only woman on board, from Friday morning till the following Monday (when) we were towed into New Orleans. I then found everything I had was ruined with water. Several small boxes (had) burst open, and the contents were lost.' What was left was saturated with water, and yet the customs officers, 'unprincipled men' she calls them, insisted on a lone woman paying $22 for the passage and luggage. Two black women helped her to wring and dry her wet belongings on the levee (river embankment) and repack them into two new containers she purchased; it was a two-day task.

The agony was by no means over:

By the time all was packed and freighted it was too late that evening to take the train, so we had to remain there all night. I made up a place on the boxes for the boys to rest on, and I sat up all night to watch my things. To tell you I was thoroughly exhausted and worn out would feebly express it. Then I fully realised the truth of that promise 'As thy day thy strength shall be'.

Before leaving New Orleans she learned that the alleged fraudster who stole her land and her money had died of yellow fever within nine hours of their fateful meeting, but she expresses no comment either way about his sudden demise.

On the long journey by train across Louisiana into the state of Mississippi and then by steamer to Alabama, she felt so sick she could scarcely stand, and the boys were still far from well. It was 4 a.m. when they arrived at Mobile, only to discover that Henry was not there to meet them. Later he said he had not received her letter. It took her two hours to find 'drays' (horse-drawn carts) to carry the family and their luggage to the boarding house where he was staying. Even though she was too unwell to eat breakfast and unable to walk, Henry suggested going to look at the house that would be their future home and tried to revive her with lemonade in a restaurant. 'I put it to my lips to drink, and that is all I knew. I dropped down and lost consciousness.' When her eyes reopened she was back in the boarding house, and two doctors standing by her bed said she had yellow fever. By nightfall the boys, their father, and his brother Edward, who was staying there too, were all prostrate with the disease and tended day and night by the doctors and four nurses. By the fifth day, Henry was so ill the doctors feared he would not live to see another sunrise.

She heard the nurses whisper that his coffin would be brought in through the window – and she would die soon after! 'I was not able to talk loud, but I wrote on a slate which was kept by my bedside that if they did not bring him on his bed to me I would go to him (even) if I died in the attempt.' His bed was brought to her. 'Whether the moving (of) him caused a reversal of the disease I know not, but the vomiting ceased, and when the doctors came in again they held up their hands in astonishment. From this time we both began to improve, and the Lord in his mercy raised us up.' The local newspapers called their cases 'the worst' Mobile had known in eight years.

Illness struck again within a fortnight. She had pleurisy and Henry started to suffer from ague so badly she feared for his reason. After six months of ups and downs the doctors told them they needed to move to the more temperate weather of the north to stay alive, and they and five English friends with families decided to become farmers in Iowa or Illinois. The steamer trip was not the end but the continuance of their difficulties. She and Henry suffered a recurrence of ague, the vessel broke down and had to be repaired, and there was a ten-day wait at St Louis for the ferry to their destination, Dubuque in Iowa. When they reached the town, nearly a month had passed since leaving Mobile. Mary Ann was offered plots of land in the best part of Dubuque and could have bought two for $100, but Henry was against it. She regrets not taking the offers, for three years later individual plots, each with a small cottage, fetched $7,000 apiece – testimony to the population growth in the Mid-West. By the time of the Smiths' arrival, European immigration had nearly trebled the population of Iowa since 1833 when American government treaties began to extinguish Indian claims to the land.

The Smiths settled on the prairie twenty-one miles west of Dubuque where Mary Ann bought eighty acres of rich agricultural land with the intention of starting a farm. Henry built a house, and they acquired cattle, a horse, pigs, and chickens, but they knew nothing about farming and made little progress. The boys seemed to like the life, despite missing their father who was away from home for weeks at a time building properties elsewhere, and in time they would be able to run the farm. In the early years various other enterprises were tried to boost the family income, beginning with a general store in the local village, Bankston, which proved to be risky because customers asked for credit or, instead of cash, offered butter, eggs and poultry, which Mary Ann had to sell in Dubuque. She petitioned successfully to open a post office, and Henry was appointed postmaster, but he was hardly ever at home and left her to run it. They might have done well, she believes, had not money been taken from the store, presumably by Henry, and seldom returned. Accumulating debt forced her to close the business.

There was one person living with the Smiths in 1850 who is not mentioned anywhere in Mary Ann's diary. The national census of that year includes an eight-year-old girl named Elizabeth Whiten in the household, but reveals nothing more about her except that she was born in Iowa, and one can only surmise that she was a local unfortunate who had been given shelter by the deeply Christian family. Oddly, she doesn't appear in the 1856 census but turns up again in the 1860, this time described as a servant with the surname amended to Whitten with two 't's.

Despite everything that had happened to the family since leaving Christchurch, Mary Ann was firmly rooted in America after four years in Iowa, and her sons were taking over the farm management in the long absences of their father. An opportunity arose to resurrect the Congregationalist faith she had followed in Christchurch, and with nine neighbours of the same persuasion, they decided to start a Congregational church.

By clubbing together and with generous help from businesspeople in Dubuque, they opened a 'nice little building', which Henry and another man erected, and obtained the services of a minister.

The Smiths' fourth year in Iowa, 1854, brought both grief and happiness. In April Mary Ann learned that her 'dear old father', Thomas Barrow, had died on 17 March at the age of seventy-one from what the death certificate describes as 'paralysis from disease of the brain'. In October his widow, Susannah Barrow, came from Christchurch 'to end her days' with their daughter and was present for a happy occasion, the marriage on 8 November of Mary Ann's elder son Thomas, now aged twenty-one, to a neighbour, Hanna Emerson. The first of their four children was born in the following August.

Hanna's father, William Emerson, was one of the most energetic workers for the new church. He taught a Bible class, superintended the Sabbath School, and also assisted in prayer meetings, but when it came to communion he would always leave. Mary Ann describes him as 'a Baptist with very strong views'; but he was probably a Unitarian - many American Congregationalists share the Unitarian rejection of certain aspects of orthodox theology - and another pointer is that he came from the east coast and was related to one of America's most controversial Nonconformists, the celebrated philosopher, essayist and poet Ralph Waldo Emerson, who resigned as a Unitarian pastor in Massachusetts in protest at the church's observance of the Lord's Supper.

The circumstances concerning Mary Ann's younger son Edward are not entirely clear from the transcript, but he left home in 1855 to fetch a girl named Mary from England with the intention of returning to America with her and her father, Joseph Bennett, early in the New Year on the steamship *Pacific*. Reports of icebergs in the North Atlantic shipping lanes deeply worried Mary Ann, who telegraphed the vessel's owners for news, and even they 'gave her up as lost', she says. The *Pacific* did disappear with the loss of all the passengers and crew, but Edward and Mary had changed their booking at the last minute and were safe on a sailing ship, the *Northumberland*. When they turned up in Iowa it was for Mary Ann 'like receiving them from the dead'. The couple married, but there seems to be no official record of the date and place of the ceremony.

The majority of the immigrants from several European countries who settled in Iowa were Catholics, and it is a sad reflection of the religious intolerance of those days that Mary Ann's Protestant neighbours were 'selling up and moving out'.

Her mother died on Christmas Eve 1856. That winter was unusually severe, and her coffin had to be carried to the grave through snow drifts up to 8ft high. No minister could be reached, and it was Thomas's father-in-law, the ever-dependable William Emerson, who stepped in and conducted the prayer for the departed. Early in the following year the schoolmistress from Christchurch was lured back to the classroom by an invitation to teach the district school, and she taught there and at another school for 'quite a number of terms'.

Mary Ann recalls 'the first mutterings of the rebellion' in the 1850s. These were the political upheavals over slavery that would lead to the shattering Civil War between the northern and southern states in 1861, during which Utah would become one of the principal breadbaskets for the North. Mary Ann's youngest son Edward, who had moved his family to another county, was subject to militia duty, and in March 1862 he enlisted in the 21st Iowa Regiment. Thomas and Hanna had also moved and were living in 'a nice little house' built by his father. Mary Ann continued to run the farm with some help and an elderly Dutchman to look after the animals.

'They were days and weeks of anxiety and suspense' she writes, and it must have been a tremendous relief when the guns ceased firing in 1865 and Edward returned home safely, but 500,000 men lay dead and the health of tens of thousands of survivors had been permanently damaged.

Some time after 1862, Henry succumbed to his wanderlust. He went to St Louis and wrote letters from there and several other places, but his deserted wife never saw him again. The last she heard was that he had taken a ship from Boston bound for England, where he told friends in London and Guernsey she was dead. Twenty-eight years passed before they learned the truth, and she received 'kind and loving letters from them all'. Her diary ends with the conciliatory words about her husband, 'I hope and trust ere he left this world he was forgiven by Him who doeth all things well, as freely as I forgave him, feeling sure his mind was unbalanced.'

Mary Ann was a great age when she died. A touching appreciation of her is made in a note that Mrs Andersen attached to the transcript. 'Great-grandmother was a valiant Christian gentlewoman who faced the many hardships of her life with courage. I am proud of the heritage she has handed down to me and only hope that I am worthy of it.'

Christchurch and Dorset have a right to be proud of her too.

14

Call of the Yukon

Stifled within the files and ledgers of a London bank and far from the fresh countryside of his native Dorset, the twenty-three year old clerk dreamed of following his doctor's advice to seek a healthier life in the open air, but William White had an even more compelling reason to quit his job; he was not earning enough to marry his fiancée Nell, otherwise known as Ellen Lydia Loaring. Reading the newspaper stories of fabulous fortunes being won in the Klondike gold rush in north-west Canada he decided to join it. So in February 1898, the pale office worker with no experience of the rough and tough world outside Victorian England sailed from Liverpool on the steamship *Huron* bound for his future in the New World. He had promised his tearful Ellen, whom he affectionately called Nell or Nelly, he would return within four years, later amended to 'soon' in correspondence, but in the event she had to wait eight years for gold on her finger.

The discoveries along the Klondike, a tributary of the Yukon River, provoked the maddest stampede in the turbulent history of gold rushes. It was sparked off by George Washington Carmack, an American with an Indian wife, who had been prospecting in the area for several years and was on the point of giving up when he and his two Indian companions, Tagish Charlie and Skookum Jim, found 'colour' (specks of gold) worth millions of dollars as they sieved the muddy waters of a Yukon creek. They arrived in Seattle with what has been described as more than a ton of gold, but whatever the quantity, it was enough to send America wild with excitement. In 1896 30,000 hopefuls joined the frenzied scramble for the elusive metal in the wilderness of mountains, lakes, cataracts and glaciers between the Canada/Alaska border and the Arctic Circle.

A further 70,000 hopefuls followed in the next two years, among them William White from the small town of Bridport, which lies within a whiff of the English Channel on the Dorset coast. His departure at the age of twenty for bustling London and a job in the headquarters of the Post Office Savings Bank may well have been inspired by the example of his father, Thomas White, who as a young man had become unhappy working in a Bridport haberdashery and left the town for the thriving potteries of Staffordshire in the English Midlands. He returned with his young wife Marion and three-year-old William, and using his newfound expertise in the pottery trade he opened a china and glass shop in Bridport in partnership with Marion. The hardworking couple struck it rich with their venture and needing room for expansion after four years, they moved further along the town's main street to a large private residence, Worcester House, which they converted into a shop.

Both William's parents came from old local families; Thomas's father of the same name worked as a shipwright in the harbour at West Bay, Bridport's outlet to the sea; Marion's father, William Churchill Rendall, was a tenant farmer and baker in a hamlet two miles away in Shipton Gorge, which is somewhat less spectacular than its name suggests - it gets the second part from the landowning de Gorges family.

Young William, the eldest of five children, absorbed the Wesleyan faith of his parents, and during his three years in the capital he attached himself to a local Methodist church and took charge of the Sunday School, like his father in Bridport. Nell, a teacher in the school, was the youngest of the four children of a noted church organist and composer, James Harwood, who had been a church organist in Crewkerne in Somerset, Dorset's neighbouring county, before moving first to St Sepulchre's in Holborn and then St Leonard's in Shoreditch, another London parish. In 1894 the Harwood family went back to the West Country and Tiverton in Devon, another county bordering Dorset. Around that time Nell took up residence in Charmouth, about seven miles from Bridport.

William revealed a graphic command of the English language in letters home and other accounts telling of his adventures, which began almost from the moment he left Liverpool. He relates how the *Huron* rolled and pitched so violently in mid-Atlantic that when he went on deck to write his first letter, he had to hang on to things to save himself from ending up in the scuppers. His rowdy companions in the second class cabins deeply offended his religious sensibilities, particularly the conduct of the women. 'There is one young girl, about twenty-two, married, and going to join her husband in Canada…my heart aches for the husband. The way that married woman behaves with some of the men is scandalous. Of course, the men are to blame to a certain extent. But when she accepts bottles of stout from one and allows another to untie her boots I think she is inexcusable.'

The worst accommodation was in the steerage class where, he believed, the passengers were mostly Jews escaping to America from the pogroms, the ethnic cleansings in Russia. One day they panicked in fear that the ship was going to sink when heavy seas smashed the bulkheads in their quarters and deluged them in tons of filthy coal from the boiler room.

White disembarked at Halifax in Nova Scotia and travelled westward by train to Vancouver on the Pacific coast of Canada, where he bought a tent, a sled, digging tools, food and cooking pan, and suitable clothing. He carried his purchases, weighing together about 800lbs, on to the *Ningchow,* an old tramp steamer that had been brought from China to join the motley fleet ferrying the army of prospectors on the 1,000-mile voyage north along the British Columbian coast to Alaska. The conditions aboard he later described in an article in a company magazine that echoed the works of novelist Jack London (*The Call of the Wild*) and poet Robert Service (*The Shooting of Dan McGrew*), both of whom he got to know personally. He wrote, 'To a youth from a God-fearing home in England, the transition to the wild and woolly was a tremendous experience. What with the drinking, gambling, hourly brawls and orgies, the tinhorns and the floozies, there was enough evil on that boat to stake a subsection in hell.'

Along the narrow Pacific strip known as the Alaskan Panhandle, the *Ningchow* called briefly at the small port of Wrangell which William described as 'about the dirtiest, filthiest, wickedest place on God's earth', and a vivid incident as the steamer was leaving convinced him that he was, indeed, a long way from home. 'The lines were casting off when a section of the crowd on the wharf threw themselves flat or ran, and simultaneously a couple of shots rang out. I saw one man crumple up and lie flat. Another, with a smoking gun in his hand, approached the body, prodded it with his foot, and walked away with an ugly snarl on his face. Our boat was on the move, and I never heard what it was all about, but it made me realise I was in a new world.'

In April he disembarked at the infamous shanty town of Skagway to begin the forty-mile trek to the Yukon and was horrified to learn that the pile of cases on the wharf contained the corpses of ten men. They had died in a couple of avalanches along the trail and were being shipped to the south for burial. Sixty or seventy of the 200 men engulfed in the disaster lost their lives. It was Palm Sunday, and the pass over the mountains was closed as a mark of respect.

He recalled:

> Skagway in 1898 and 99 was probably the greatest sink-hole of iniquity the North American continent has ever known, a fact borne out by many contemporary writings. Wild and lawless beyond conception, the infamous Soapy Smith and his gang were in full control, and robberies and killings were a nightly occurrence. High-powered crooks and denizens of the underworld plied their calling, brazenly and with impunity, for the US Marshal was their friend and got his 'cut' from all.

The notorious 'Soapy' was Jefferson Randolph Smith, whose gun ruled over the saloons, dance halls and gambling dens in Alaska's largest town at that time, which had mushroomed from a mere two in 1887 to 20,000 in ten hectic years. One of the swindles by which Soapy and his henchmen conned unwary prospectors out of their cash and hard-won gold dust involved a charge of $5 apiece to send a telegram home – but the telegraph did not exist. Finally, Soapy was challenged by an angry mob of citizens, and a gunfight exploded between him and a brave town official, Frank Reid. Both men died from their wounds, and Soapy's nine month reign of terror ended in pools of blood.

On the voyage from England, White had invested £70 in a syndicate of nine prospectors who agreed to share the proceeds of any gold finds. They pooled their resources and set out from Skagway with six donkeys, one mule, twenty-three dogs, sleds, a boat and two canoes on the longer but less arduous of the two trails to the goldfields. They trudged up the valley of the Skagway River towards the mountains and White Horse Pass nearly 3,000ft above sea-level on the US/Canada border, and from the summit they descended to a swamp which took them four days to get through. The temperatures fell well below zero at night but rose to 70 or 80°C during the day, and three times the loaded sled that White was driving with the dogs fell through thawing snow. The flooding that followed rose above the heads of the donkeys, and they had to be pulled out with ropes. One night a thief stole the donkeys and tried to sell them on the trail back to Alaska, but the animals were detained by the US Customs men for some breach of regulations and returned to the syndicate. The terrible conditions were taking their toll of the animals; one mule fell sick and had to be shot, and the donkeys were reduced to four.

The men camped on several feet of snow, laying their beds on the boughs of balsam trees and blankets. About this time, William saw himself in a mirror for the first time in weeks and was astonished by the whiskery, nut-brown face that stared back at him. The city pallor had vanished, and he felt fitter and fatter than ever before. As the camp cook, he had to melt snow to obtain pure water, because the rivers and streams were polluted with the putrefying corpses of pack animals which had been driven to their deaths in the prospectors' desperate haste to the goldfields. Three thousand animals perished on what became known as Dead Horse Trail, causing a stench that drew swarms of voracious mosquitoes, and William and his comrades were covered with bumps.

Despite the arduous life, William retained his sense of humour. In one letter he jokes that his cooking prowess had not yet killed anyone in the party, adding 'as hard as I've tried!' In fact, they were eating surprisingly well. He served porridge and fried bacon for breakfast and for dinner bacon and beans, followed by a dessert such as treacle pudding, jam roly-poly, baked rice pudding and jam, apple dumplings, stewed apricots, peaches, or prunes, figs or raisin pudding.

Again his English humour emerges in his letters. He varies the dinner monotony of bacon and beans by serving beans and bacon, he tells one of his sisters. 'Oh, you should see this boy – what a saving I shall be for Nellie. She won't need to keep a cook, the cook will keep her, and she'll be parlour maid and have nothing to do with the kitchen.'

Inwardly, he was deeply concerned about his fiancée and asked his sister to visit her as much as possible:

> I don't want her to go out to business again, if it can be avoided, for she really cannot stand it, but if she is staying at home for any length of time it will make her miserable. I do feel anxious about her but leave you to do all you can to cheer her up 'til the prodigal returns. Tell her and mother that it won't be long now, as you can get to the Yukon in much less than a week when the ice breaks.

The correspondence between William and his betrothed has sadly not survived, but one wonders what Nell thought of the phrase 'it won't be long now' as the weeks stretched to months and then years.

After the thirty-three mile slog up the valley from Skagway and the steep, treacherous mountain descent, the travel-stained and weary party saw amid the snowcapped mountains the clear and refreshing waters of Lake Bennett. It was

Sunday, and William and two other members of the syndicate held an impromptu service and sang hymns to God, while an unheeding congregation, camped among hundreds of tents and two or three log cabins, prayed for a vision of gold. About two o'clock one morning, he woke up in his tent to find an agitated female clasping his feet and crying, 'Oh, mister, oh mister, what shall I do?' She claimed to have seen a huge bear only about a hundred yards away. Whatever the truth of her story, he soberly calmed her down, and she hailed him as her saviour.

Some of the prospectors were building boats for the 500 mile paddle to the Yukon and the capital, Dawson City, closer to the Arctic Circle. William and his comrades assembled 'a respectable fleet', including a flat-bottomed boat to carry their animals. They had lost a large amount of provisions along the way and were short of ready cash, but they traded with the local Indians. They had also lost two of their number who withdrew from the syndicate. The little flotilla set out at the end of June, but the next day a storm blew them on to the rocky shore of the lake. Desperately, the men jumped into the water to manoeuvre the craft into a sheltered bay. William was washed off his feet by the waves, but Stansfield had stayed on the boat and grabbed him before he was swept away. After beaching the boat to repair some leaks, the party paddled on to Lake Tagish and rested at a North-west Mounted Police post. William saw four Indians manacled and chained together and guessed they were probably going to be shot for murdering a Klondike miner and wounding another. In actual fact, crime was comparatively low in the Canadian territory compared with Skagway on the US Alaskan side of the border.

It was now well into July, and William was hoping to be home in England by Christmas, rich from the gold he was confident they would find. He and another member guarded the kit while the other two, Jack Williams and Stansfield, went ahead to gauge the prospects in the Lake Atlin area. Four days later, Williams staggered into the camp completely exhausted. The pair had got lost, and as Stansfield was too tired to find his way back to the camp, he stayed in the forest despite the presence of numerous bears. Williams recovered, and he and William hacked through the forest to rescue Stansfield. He had survived by shooting birds for food, but was suffering from burns, having trod on hot ashes in bare feet.

In August the Klondike stampede ended as suddenly as it began, but many of the diggers rushed north following reports of another rich find. The syndicate hastily set out on the seventy mile trek to Pine Creek. An Indian misdirected them, and they found themselves paddling down a fast-running stream that was occasionally blocked by driftwood, and each time they had to unload their belongings and carry them and the canoes along the bank. Headwinds on Lake Atlin whipped the waves into rollers and forced them to spend a wasted day on an island. Provisions were running low by the time they reached Pine Creek, but they were excited by the news they had longed to hear: gold was being discovered in large quantities. They staked claims to 'spacers', alluvial deposits mixed with grains and nuggets of gold, and William named his first claim 'Bridport Spacer'. As it happened, the claim next to his belonged not to some grizzled 'Sourdough' (Klondike prospector) but to the son of an aristocrat, Sir Richard Cartwright, who

William White, the gold-rush pioneer who became head of securities for a Canadian bank. (Yukon Archives)

was Canada's Minister for Trade and Commerce and later became acting Premier.

For the first time in months they were able to sleep in comfortable accommodation at a police camp. They were warmly welcomed by the Mounties whom they had helped on a couple of occasions, once when they gave needed food to one of their patrols and again when they saved a Mountie from drowning in freezing water after his canoe capsized.

Buoyed up with rising expectations of a lucky strike, the syndicate planned to build a large cabin before the winter set in and open it as a restaurant. William rubbed his hands at the prospect of 'five to ten thousand diners paying a dollar at time for a meal' when winter ice drove them off the goldfields. Another delight was his first letters from Dorset, one from his sister Lily in Bridport and the other from Nell.

The finding of two large nuggets worth $42 and $45 encouraged plans to move further north to check out a new strike, but the four-man syndicate was beginning to break up. Stansfield's 'mad schemes and actions' were proving unbearable, and the syndicate, identified by the initials SYS, was becoming known as 'Stansfield's Yukon Swindle'. One member, named Swann, left to work on his own. William resigned and formed a partnership with Jack Williams, and Stansfield was left the only survivor of the original venture.

By the time of the break-up, William owned three mines and shares in two others. He and Jack bought a corner plot in Atlin City and built the hoped-for log cabin which was completed by the onset of winter. William was digging up small quantities of gold in his claims, one of which was a hole 9ft deep, and sent a small sample in a letter home. On a twelve day trip to the O'Connell River district with Jack, William secured good claims on three rivers and named them Lily of Bridport and, simply, Nell.

As Christmas approached, William gathered forty homesick Britons together to observe a traditional Christmas. The pious William, acting as secretary, recalled that Christmas Eve was a beautiful night. 'The moon shone forth in the heavens with a lustre altogether unusual, even in this country with its glorious atmosphere, whilst the snow underfoot was as crisp and dry as a well-cooked biscuit.' Seven of the group sang carols at various homes in the town and were offered hot coffee and cakes, and the Atlin Hotel invited them inside for hot toddy – William, a tee-totaller, accepted cigars instead. It was gone 3 a.m. when the carollers retired to bed.

Weeks later the White family in Bridport and Nell pining in Charmouth, received letters from William which helped them to imagine the scene at the Dickensian dinner that night. The log cabin he and Jack had built, crouched deep in snow blanched by a fluorescent moon, and the windows glowed orange from the warm light within challenging the frozen air. The grizzled miners, thinking of distant homes, sat down to a menu as traditional as they could possibly make it, their bearded faces lit up by flickering candles, their shadows moving on rough timber walls decorated with greenery, guns and the Canadian flag, and four women bustled in Victorian skirts serving the hungry men. Meals that must have been cooked and prepared in the most crude of circumstances, included pies, stews, puddings of moose, grouse, rabbit, followed by plum pudding, cakes, stewed fruits and, of course, minced pies. With the utensils they had brought with them, the miners ate in total silence for two and a half hours, except for the occasional sigh of contentment.

'But such a state of things could not last forever,' William wrote, 'and after eleven o'clock the intensity of purpose written on every face began to give place to a benign and self-complacent affability that soon became as hilarious and genial as can be found only in a John Bull party…and the meal that began with a rigid silence ended amidst laughter and jollity that sounded as English as one could wish.' The men (here the modern feminist reader should look away!) the men retired to a drug store for a smoke and a chat and no doubt a liquid or two, while the women sat down to what was left of the meal. The abstemious William stayed with them to help with the clearing up.

The others returned to the cabin, and at midnight they all drank a toast to Queen Victoria and sang the national anthem to the accompaniment of a scratch band consisting of a violin, clarinet and guitar. Songs, further toasts and speeches followed 'and most present felt a lump in their throat whilst we drank to absent friends at home'. The party went on until 6.30 the next morning. 'So ended a Christmas dinner and party that will live in the memories of all present,' wrote William, hastening to reassure his family that although they were men of all sorts and conditions 'there was perfect gentlemanliness throughout and not one word or action that the most prudish could have regretted, and three of the ladies present (one must have gone home) were able to stay to the finish and have a real good time'.

Although the miners and the women were able momentarily to forget the rigour of their lives, danger was always present in the Klondike. A much-respected doctor disappeared, and William feared he had wandered from the trail, and the discovery of bones indicated he had been eaten by ravenous wolves. New Year's Day began in glorious weather but ended in tragedy. Lake Atlin had frozen over during the night and many men went skating on the ice, keeping close to the shore, but two drunks tried to walk to an island and fell into the freezing water. Two other men rushed to the rescue with a canoe but all four drowned. William, a member of the jury at the inquest, had witnessed the scene, and his abhorrence of liquor deepened.

He and Jack failed to find gold in significant quantities. They tried other ventures to make money; harvesting and selling hay for animal fodder, chopping lumber for sale, and running a roadhouse to feed travellers on the trail, but they all ended in failure and the final break-up of the partnership. By the following spring William was alone in Whitehorse town with fifty cents in his pocket, his dreams of fortune having faded into bitter disappointment. Then luck came his way. A railway had been built from Skagway, and he was abjectly watching a train depart when a temporary job was offered to him, and in less than an hour he was standing behind the counter in the Whitehorse branch of the Canadian Bank of Commerce.

He must have reflected on the irony of his situation; he had travelled thousands of miles to escape from a bank, and here he was back at work in one. In a matter of weeks his job became permanent, and in fact his new 'temporary' career lasted for the rest of his working life.

Life was still fraught with danger in the Yukon. William heard of an armed gunman who walked into a Skagway bank and demanded a large sum of money. The counter clerk appeared to accede, went towards the safe, and then dashed towards a door shouting to his fellow clerks to duck. The startled robber fired wildly, hitting no-one, but the noise detonated a stick of dynamite in his pocket, and the explosion killed him and injured two of the staff. Gold dust contained in a large canister on the counter was scattered all over the room. Clearing up the mess the staff discovered an ounce more of the precious metal than was listed in their records; they concluded that it must have collected under the floorboards over the years.

Promoted to branch manager at Skagway, William found a thumb of the would-be robber preserved in a bottle of alcohol and the bones of other parts in a mouldy sack behind logs in a woodshed. William carried them in a new sack to a doctor friend and tipped them on to his office floor. 'They were in a poor state of preservation, worm-eaten and mildewed,' wrote William. 'The doctor picked out one or two of interest to him, and I took the skull. The rest we gathered up and threw into his stove, so in the end much of the robber was actually cremated!' The skull stayed in the bank for some years until William presented it to the local dentist, who placed it on his mantelpiece. And that was the last William heard of it.

The Canadian Bank of Commerce closed the Skagway branch and over the years appointed William to branches on Vancouver Island, and in Manitoba, British Columbia, Ontario, and Vancouver. During a brief visit to Bridport, he told Nell that the bank's employees were expected to remain single until they were earning above their current salary, which was too low in his case, and she agreed to the postponement of their marriage pending his promotion. The situation was ironic, of course, because this was his reason for leaving London to seek his fortune in the Yukon. Nell must have been bitterly disappointed, and this time William told his employers he was going to marry anyway, whether they fired him or not, and they promoted him to accountant with a higher salary. One wonders why he had not been bold and presented this ultimatum before.

Nell hurried to make arrangements to join him in Canada after faithfully waiting eight years for the happy day. She was now twenty-eight. Foul weather delayed

The remains of a Skagway bank. Clearing up the mess, the staff discovered an ounce *more* of the precious metal than was listed in their records. (Yukon Archives)

the Atlantic crossing for four days, and when Nell arrived in Montreal with her wedding trousseau, the longed-for marriage ceremony had to be rushed through. The minister was in a hurry to go on holiday, so the reunited lovers stood in their every-day clothes in his home as he pronounced them man and wife. The white wedding dress Nell had lovingly made all those years ago lay in a trunk back at her hotel and was never worn.

After a honeymoon breakfast of sausages, the newly-weds left next day for Fernie in British Columbia where William was employed in the local branch of the Canadian Bank of Commerce. Over the ensuing years his promotions switched their home to Manitoba and then Ontario, and when William retired in 1932 he was the bank's Custodian of Securities in Vancouver. With the notion of spending their retirement years in Bridport, he and Nell spent a winter with his parents, but they missed the creature comforts of Canada, particularly the central heating, and went back to Vancouver.

The courage and tenacity of the Sourdoughs who risked their lives in the Yukon have been immortalised by novelist Jack London (who had been one of the prospectors) and poet Robert Service, but there can be few accounts more moving than those of the Dorset Sourdough. Full versions of his letters were published in 1990 in a book *Writing Home to Dorset from the Yukon* by T.D. Saunders, to whom this author is greatly indebted. In retrospect, one can see that by the time White reached the goldfields the best claims had been established, and by August many of the stampeders were leaving, disconsolate and penniless. Perhaps, when the syndicate began falling apart, White should have given up or moved on with an even greater gold rush to Nome in Alaska. Perhaps, perhaps…but for him and the patient, loyal Nell the story ended happily.

Meet the Family

William was not the only member of the White family to 'discover' the New World; both his brothers joined him in Canada. Harold became a salesman in Vancouver and later moved to Florida in the US. Albert started a farm under a scheme that William arranged for him, but it was not successful, and Albert returned after one summer to run a dairy in Bridport in the 1920s and 1930s. While William was in the Yukon his mother's uncle, Charles Rendall, the son of a blacksmith trained as a tailor, but at the age of twenty-two he turned to farming after emigrating to Minnesota and, following the family tradition became a Methodist preacher. He died two days before his 100th birthday. When he and his wife Ann celebrated their diamond wedding anniversary in July 1914, more than 100 descendants were present, but one of their twelve children was missing. Job Rendall had gone south with the Wisconsin Volunteers in the Civil War and succumbed to malaria in Arkansas in May 1863.

William and Nell became the proud parents of three children, a boy and two daughters, one of whom, Doreen, was interviewed in Vancouver for a BBC programme on the Klondike gold rush, televised in 1996, in which she described her mother as 'a sweet girl'.

Historic Bridport

William White's birthplace has a recorded history going back at least to the eleventh century when the Norman conquerors compiled a list of their spoils, the Domesday Book, and included Bridport. The area had been known to the Romans and later the Saxons, and the thirteenth-century monarch Henry III granted Bridport a charter which gave the inhabitants more power over their own affairs. Fourteen years later, in 1274, the town became a seaport with the construction of a harbour at West Bay. As England's marine strength grew through the Middle Ages, so did a Bridport industry, using locally grown flax and hemp to make ropes and nets for fishing boats and the navy fleet. The business still thrives.

A stranger walked boldly into the George Inn one day in the seventeenth century. Charles II was fleeing into exile on the Continent after his army was defeated by Oliver Cromwell's troops at the Battle of Worcester in 1651, but after seeing the Bridport streets crowded with Republican soldiers, the king and his companions rode away.

Some other unwelcome visitors arrived in June 1685 and took possession of the town. They were cavalry supporting the Duke of Monmouth, the Protestant eldest of Charles II's eleven illegitimate children, who had invaded Lyme Regis further along the Dorset coast with the intention of taking the crown from Catholic James II, but the Bridport militia chased the horsemen away. It was the first defeat of the doomed Monmouth insurrection.

15

A Life in the Forest

Cod fishing on Newfoundland Banks left a legacy that would one day threaten the future of the island's other natural resource - the forests. Fishermen from Dorset and the West of England as well as the Continent hacked the spruce and fir along the coast for wood to construct their mooring stages, erect shelters and repair their boats. The discarded brushwood was burned without heed for the danger of forest fires, and as early as 1619, according to one record, '5,000 acres of forest were maliciously burned by fishers in the Bay of Conception with many more thousands of acres burned and destroyed by them in these last 20 years'. With the advent of permanent settlements by both the British and French and the coming of the lumber and pulp industries, large areas were left barren, particularly the Avalon peninsular in the south-east where the Christchurch squire, Lord Baltimore, had established his settlements. Avalon reminded one well known travel writer in the 1980s of the Canadian Arctic, an impression emphasised by the herds of up to 100 caribou he could see from the main road.

The whole of the forest was in peril by 1877 when a seventeen-year-old English youth from Dorset stepped ashore in search of a new life in Newfoundland. Thomas Howe can have known little, if anything, about the care and protection of forest trees, but he became involved and learned his craft well. In nearly fifty years devoted to conservation, he pioneered modern methods of forestry and was regarded as an acknowledged authority. In 1905, his twenty-ninth year, his expertise had been recognised by his appointment under new legislation as Newfoundland's first Chief Woods Ranger in charge of all the forests, both Crown and private. His role included fire prevention and control and came not a moment too soon, for a new menace had arrived - steam trains linking the west and east coasts of the island. Their cinders had scorched more than 2 million acres of forest along the track. As a government official responsible for investigating forest fires, Howe rode on the trains and, according to one relative, he sometimes took his family with him for the ride. His task was to ensure that fire protection measures were being observed, but the railwaymen were not always cooperative, and on one day Howe recorded sixty-two fires in six miles. The total rose to 1,193 in 1912, over 90 per cent caused by the trains. 'More timber had been destroyed by fire than could be sawn into lumber in a hundred years.' he reported, estimating that the 6,000 square miles of burned land

Thomas Howe, pioneer of conservation and sustainable methods of forestry, and Newfoundland's first Chief Woods Ranger. (Thomas Howe Demonstration Forest Foundation)

could have yielded prepared timber worth more than $300,000, a considerable sum in the early 1900s.

Howe was diligent in chasing offenders. *A History of the Newfoundland Forest Protection Association* by W.J. Carroll, former Director of the Canadian Forest Service, relates that on one occasion Howe came across a prominent Newfoundland politician burning brushwood on his farm. Told it was unsafe and illegal under the Forest Fires Act, the legislator retorted, 'My man, don't you know I could have that Act changed at any time?' Although Howe must have flinched at the demeaning 'my man', he replied coolly, 'But, sir, you haven't changed it yet,' and had him charged – and fined.

Nothing is known about Howe's childhood, who his parents were, or even what part of Dorset he came from, though research through ten parish records in which his surname occurs does suggest that he might have been born the child of a twenty-three year old servant in the town of Blandford Forum, in the north of the county. Another possibility is the village of Buckland Newton and his father could have been a shepherd. Or could he have been one of the children from local poorhouses in Wimborne Minster, Christchurch, Wareham and elsewhere? Newfoundland records reveal only that he was born in Dorset and landed at Brooklyn in Bonavista Bay, one of the Dorset settlements on the island's north-east coast in 1877. It is certain that at the age of twenty-two he married a local girl, Anna Jane Stares, and they had three sons, one of whom lived only five months. Sadly, Anna died in 1904 only five years after the wedding. At the age of forty-four Howe married again, this time to Selina Andrews who was eighteen and a sister of the wife of his youngest son, William. They made their home at Port Blandford, his work-base in Newfoundland, and raised a daughter.

Howe was promoted to senior warden over millions of acres of forest stretching 350 miles across Newfoundland, from the Atlantic to the Gulf of St Lawrence off the Canadian mainland, and was given four assistants jointly funded by his employers and industry. They patrolled the railway line on foot, looking out for telltale smoke and flames which they tackled with pails and shovels. Later they were equipped with a little more sophistication - handpumps and four-wheeled vehicles called velocipedes that travelled on the lines and were worked by hand – but it was still a far cry from the advanced fire-fighting armoury of today. Fire towers keep a constant watch over the forests with radio, telephones, and instruments that pinpoint trouble spots with accuracy. Specially-equipped aircraft are used to dump water on serious outbreaks, and there are more than 1,000 professional and support staff.

British and French disputes over fishing and settlement rights were finally ended in 1713 with the Treaty of Utrecht, which formally brought the War of Spanish Accession to a close and ceded Newfoundland to Britain, but the troubles of the island's principal earner were not over. Ups and downs in market prices for fish led to national insolvency on three occasions in the nineteenth and twentieth centuries, but despite an offer of a comforting embrace by the Canadian Confederation, the small population of mainly British descent stayed proud and independent until 1949, when the island colony finally became, with the addition of the coastal region of mainland Labrador, the tenth province of Canada.

Through anxious times, Howe repeatedly drew attention to the island's other natural resource in his annual reports to the government and regretted that greater interest was not being taken in the conservation of the forests, which he described as a valuable source of wealth obtained from ground too poor to produce anything but trees. 'There is not a country in the world where forests are so little respected and protected as the forests of the colony,' he complained.

Finally, in 1910 Howe sat with six government ministers, including the Premier and representatives of land owners and industry, and together they set up an organisation to save the forest. Among its aims were the undertaking of silvicultural training and research and forest wildlife and insect surveys. The new service was a promising step towards Howe's dream, but it looked threatened in the 1920s by yet another of Newfoundland's periodic bouts of economic restraint, and he worried that the financial axe would cut into his staff, but in a three-hour discussion with the Prime Minister, Walter Munroe, he was assured that this would not happen.

Personal tragedy came in 1933 when his second wife, Selina, died at the age of sixty-six. She was laid to rest in Blandford Port, and a year later he joined her, having lived eighty-four years since his birth in Dorset. In the same year, 1934, his life's dream was fulfilled with the formation of a new organisation dedicated to saving the forests. The Newfoundland Forest Protection Association introduced training in silviculture, including the protection of wildlife and the study of parasitic insects attacking the trees, and at Gander in 1995 the association opened an educational centre in the forest to increase public awareness of its woodland heritage. Two of Howe's descendants serve on the board of directors of the association which set up a training centre and named it after him. The Thomas Howe Demonstration Forest is a fitting memorial to a Dorset man who devoted half a century of his life to saving the forests of Newfoundland.

Visitors can find the training centre in the east central part of the island on Gander Lake, which has seen other noteworthy events. In 1901 Gander received the first transatlantic wireless message, which was transmitted from Cornwall by the pioneer of wireless telegraphy, Marconi, who had conducted some of his early experiments in Dorset. In June 1919, two Royal Air Force pilots, Alcock and Brown, set off in a wartime bomber for the first successful non-stop Atlantic flight and landed in an Irish bog. In the Second World War, Gander was the takeoff point for American aircraft joining the Allied war effort in Europe, an historic event which is marked by a monument to the crews' courage, an actual Lockheed Hudson bomber.

The 'New-Founde Land' as it was known by the ancients, was first colonised by the Vikings in about AD 1000 and visited in 1497 by Cabot, acting for the English who formally recognised it as a Crown colony in 1583.

16

A Legend in Her Time

The helicopter headed for Minterne Magna and descended on the manor house lawn where Edward, Lord Digby, was waiting with his wife, Lady Dione, to greet his elder sister, the United States' ambassador to France. Pamela Harriman had flown from Paris that morning and was beginning her visit to Britain with a brief call on her childhood home. It was to be her last, for a few months later the energetic seventy-six year old collapsed in the French capital from a fatal brain haemorrhage.

Her death the following day, 5 February 1997, unleashed the London newspapers from the British libel laws, and the obituaries smacked their lips over the more sensational aspects of her remarkable career. *The Guardian* related that 'the list of prominent men known to have shared her bed reads like a *Who's Who* of the century', while the paper's Washington correspondent observed that 'seldom since the days of Madame de Pompadour had a woman so publicly used her sensual wiles to win the fame, fortune and public prominence that she always felt was her due'. For *The Independent*, her career 'forms a fascinating bridge between the rumbustious eighteenth century and its rather more vulgar twentieth-century descendant, the airport best-seller'. The *Times* was satisfied that she was 'one of the great courtesans of her age'.

For all this journalistic hyperbole, it was not the extra-marital amours but her three marriages that took the daughter of Dorset nobility to the social and political heights of the United States, where she reigned as the uncrowned queen of Washington society and contributed with money and dedication to installing President Clinton in the White House.

Pamela Digby's fascination with the rich and powerful had begun to grip in earnest after her marriage to Winston Churchill's soldier son Randolph early on in the Second World War, and then a divorce that led to a series of post-war romantic interludes with the fast and famous on the Continent. She settled in America with her second husband, the Hollywood and Broadway producer Leland Hayward, and after his death her wartime lover and third husband, wealthy diplomat and business tycoon Averell Harriman, opened the door to the corridors of power in the American capital.

She was born to respectability and privilege as a descendant of the Digby aristocracy. Her father was the First World War hero Colonel Edward Kenelm

Digby, a product of an exclusive public school, Eton, and later Sandhurst officer training academy. While still in his twenties he commanded a battalion of the Coldstream Guards in France and emerged from the slaughter with his life and the Distinguished Service Order, the Military Cross and Bar and the Croix de Guerre. Shortly before the armistice in 1918, the tall, handsome officer fell in love with a nurse, the Honourable Constance Aberdare, who was caring for the sick and injured in a London hospital, and they married in the following year and set up home at Farnborough in Hampshire. Pamela was the eldest of four children. She was born on 20 March 1920, the year that their father inherited the title and Dorset estate of his deceased father, the tenth Baron Digby.

The eleventh of the Digby line had already accepted an appointment as Military Secretary to the Governor-General of Australia, and two and a half years elapsed before he and his family moved into the four-storey mansion at Minterne Magna, where the only boy, Edward, was born in 1924 and Jacquetta in 1928. Here, amid acres of farmland and woods, the four children enjoyed an idyllic lifestyle at the top of the county's social tree. Their father and mother immersed themselves in the agricultural and equine activities of Dorset, and the house echoed to lively talk on farm-lore and horses and the happy sound of hunt balls – father Edward was Master of Foxhounds for the Cattistock Hunt. From an early age Pamela entered enthusiastically into the horsy world, riding ponies for miles across the green hills and competing in shows with other members of her family. The rosettes and certificates they won lined the walls of the Minterne stables.

Brother Edward recalls:

> Pam always enjoyed life, a typical country life, and was a very good horsewoman. She was marvellous at shows and jumped in the International at Olympia (the prestigious London arena) and also in the Royal Bath and West and in lots of local shows such as the Dorchester and the Melplash. Whereas my second sister Sheila enjoyed hunting more, Pam was always the showgirl and rode beautifully. She show-jumped a tiny pony called Stardust that did a clear round at Olympia when every fence was above the animal's withers [shoulders]. She had an Arab pony called Poppy that ran away with me, I remember, and only Pam could readily control her. Pam was very determined, always very competitive and liked things well done, she liked to win.

Edward believes that Pamela's consuming desire to succeed stemmed from their mother's side of the family which bred 'some formidable females'. Constance was the youngest, and her great-grandfather was John Singleton Copley, the famous American painter. Contance came from a social and political heredity that could hardly be more different from her husband's. Her grandfather, Henry Austin Bruce, was the elected Member of Parliament for the coal and iron town of Aberdare in South Wales, and his zeal as a reforming Home Secretary in Gladstone's Liberal Government between 1869 and 1873 was recognised with a barony which he named after his constituency. His seat in the House of Lords passed to his heir, the second Lord Aberdare, who had six children.

Her husband was born in the Digby residence in London's fashionable Eaton Square, grew up on the Dorset estate, and eventually occupied his father's staunchly Conservative seat in the Upper House. For twenty-three years he served in the honourable corps of gentlemen-at-arms, the sovereign's ceremonial bodyguard, and was installed a Knight of the Garter, Europe's oldest order of knighthood. He was awarded the Freedom of the City of London, and his considerable expertise in plant cultivation was recognised by his appointment as President of the Royal Horticultural Society. For twelve years, until his death in 1962, he was Lord Lieutenant of Dorset, a position his father had held and which required him to represent the sovereign at functions and ceremonies in the county and act as official escort for visiting members of the royal family.

From Pamela's aristocratic background there would be every excuse for believing that she was nurtured in the English stiff-necked tradition, judging for instance by a 1930s photograph of the Digby parents and the two older girls at Minterne House. Father sits on the steps with mother, Pam, and younger sister Jaquetta (see image No.10 in central section).

The stifling formality, if that existed, could perhaps explain Pamela's eagerness to leave Dorset, but brother Edward told me he disagreed with such a conclusion. 'I don't think they were all that formal, except that life was more formal in those days. There were at least fourteen in-house staff, and that goes back to the eighteenth century when there was great rural unemployment and labour was cheap.'

Despite the political rumblings on the Continent, the Digbys continued their traditional ways in peaceful England. They rode to hounds, sent their young to boarding schools, and holidayed abroad with moneyed friends in the pre-package era. Pamela was tutored at home in the things a nicely brought-up girl should know – correct English, maths, history and needlework – before being packed off to boarding school. To be 'finished' she was lodged with carefully selected hosts in Munich and Paris. In Munich, the Hitler supporter Unity Mitford introduced her to Adolf. By 1938 Pamela was ready for the debutante circus; the 'gels' who stared wide-eyed from full-page portraits in the society glossies danced coyly into the dawn with suitable prospects at matchmaking balls in London and the Home Counties - and their mothers went too.

When Pamela reached driving age her father bought her a Jaguar, which whisked her to weekends away from parental watchfulness, particularly to Kent, where a girlfriend's American mother, Lady Baillie, owned moated Leeds Castle and entertained leaders of business, politics, theatre and the arts. Their worldly conversations made Pamela conscious of the callowness of the downy scions she partnered in London ballrooms and socialised with at the Henley rowing regatta and the Royal Ascot race meeting. Her brother does not find her reaction so extraordinary. 'Like many girls she was attracted to powerful and older men, and in Pamela's case it was a family characteristic. Both her sisters married men older than themselves, and I married a woman younger than me.' However, he disputes the assertion of American biographer Christopher Ogden in *Life of the Party* (which the mature Pamela refused to authorise) that she was finding country life boring. Edward is sure she always loved Dorset, even though her sports car allowed her to indulge the youthful urge to explore the adult world on her own. She had tasted some of that enticing world already, having stayed on the Continent and been to the US and Canada with her parents, and now the seductive pull of wealth and influence was overwhelming.

The outbreak of war in September 1939 burst on the Digby household like a bomb, and they responded instinctively to the patriotic call. Father was summoned to the War Office and promoted to the rank of Colonel, mother took charge of the women soldiers of the Auxiliary Territorial Service in Dorset as Lieutenant-Colonel, and daughter Sheila also joined the ATS. Pamela found a job with the Foreign Office in London using her facility with the language of Britain's French allies. The Digbys had to move out of Minterne House with their furniture and belongings in 1940 to make way for a naval hospital that had been bombed out of Portland, the navy base on the Dorset coast.

In the so-called 'phoney war' before the German air-raids began, Pamela found the capital an exciting place in spite of (or perhaps because of) the blackout, sandbagged public buildings, anti-aircraft guns and trenches in the parks, barrage balloons hovering in the sky, uniforms proliferating on the streets, and civilians going around with a small cardboard box on string containing their gasmask. Social life went on, and West End theatres, restaurants and nightclubs remained open. Out of the blue Pamela received a telephone call from Randolph Churchill who, as a reservist officer, was joining his father's old regiment, the Fourth Hussars.

He had been given her name by a mutual friend, and they may have met as children before the war because Winston's signature occurs in the visitor's book at Minterne House. In fact, the mansion was the Churchill family home under lease from Winchester College for 135 years until Admiral Robert Digby bought it in 1768. Before inviting Pamela to join him at the noted Quaglino's restaurant, young Churchill asked her, with what Anita Leslie describes in her biography *Cousin Randolph* as 'insufferable arrogance', what she looked like. She replied, 'Red-headed and rather fat, but Mummy says that puppy fat disappears.' They dined, and one or two nights later he proposed. Their engagement was announced in the next three days, and on 4 October they were married at the society church of St John's in London's Smith Square. She was nineteen, he was twenty-eight, and the war was four weeks old.

The marriage was to be short-lived. Randolph had sought a wife in a hurry, Edward believes, because he was a soldier and life could be short. 'He wanted an heir, I'm sure that is the short answer. He could be very attractive if he wanted to be; I liked him very much.' Anita Leslie thought her cousin had been spoilt in his upbringing, while Ogden bluntly describes him as a drinker, gambler and woman-chaser. It was an unhappy marriage doomed to failure.

At the time of the wedding, Pamela's father-in-law was the First Lord of the Admiralty, the responsibility he had previously held in the First World War. He was vigorously combating the U-boat and mine threats to the nation's marine lifelines in May 1940 when the Germans invaded the Low Countries, and Prime Minister

Pamela Digby competing in a
Dorset gymkhana. (Southern
Newspapers)

Neville Chamberlain, who had appeased Adolph Hitler before the war, bowed to
public pressure and resigned. He was succeeded by Churchill, who had long warned
the nation of the Nazi menace, and moved into the Cabinet Office at 10 Downing
Street on the swell of public acclaim. His wife, Clementine, recruited Pamela to assist
them at dinners and receptions, and the Dorset girl quickly learned the feminine
skill of putting eminent men at ease without being obtrusive. During the nightly air
raids, the Churchills would take to the bombproof shelter, a wine cellar under the
building, and Pamela would sleep on the lower half of the bunk bed while Winston
occupied the upper half. According to Ogden, Pamela afterwards joked that she had
one Churchill above her and another inside her – she was several months' pregnant.

She obliged with Randolph's wishes on 10 October at Chequers, the official
country residence of British Premiers, and the boy was christened Winston Spencer
Churchill after his famous grandfather. Away from the London blitz, a nanny was
appointed to look after the baby at the out-of-town home of Lord Beaverbrook, the
Canadian owner of *The Daily Express* and a member of the War Cabinet. She was left
free to host important wartime guests at No. 10 and Chequers, and was blossoming
into a very attractive young woman with an engaging figure that did not pass
unnoticed by the American railroad millionaire and diplomat, W. Averell Harriman.
President Roosevelt had sent him to Britain to expedite the Lend-Lease agreement
under which the United States, while remaining neutral, would supply the military
aid that Britain urgently needed. After Randolph was posted to the Middle East early
in February 1941, Averell and Pamela became lovers; she was twenty-one and he
fifty with a wife (his second) in New York and two daughters by his first. No secret
was made of the affair, and the Churchills gave no outward sign of disapproval, even

though their cuckolded son was abroad serving his country in a theatre of war. Her parents, a strictly conventional couple, must have known of her infidelity.

At twenty-one, Pamela was no longer the gauche maiden from the sticks but a slim beauty moving gracefully between the two camps in the Lend-Lease negotiations, and there is speculation that she learned information from the American side that was useful intelligence for Churchill and Beaverbrook. She was with Averell and other dinner guests at Chequers on 7 December 1941 when the news broke of the Japanese attack on Pearl Harbour that launched the US into joining Britain in the war.

Randolph returned to England in the spring of 1942 to recuperate from a crushed vertebra which tormented him for the rest of his life. He had been promoted to Major with a staff job in Cairo, but having been trained as a commando he volunteered for a daring raid on the enemy-held port of Benghazi in Libya. The operation was successful, but on the desert road back to Cairo, the Ford utility he was in collided with another army vehicle and overturned. The war correspondent of *The Daily Telegraph* was killed and others were hurt, Randolph among them. Despite the injury he parachuted into Yugoslavia some months later to share the dangers facing the Tito partisans. For all his reputed faults as a philanderer, reckless gambler and rowdy in his cups, he was a brave and good soldier.

Not surprisingly, Randolph and Pamela quarrelled while he was in England. Edward observed:

> Randolph certainly thought Pamela ought to stay in the country and look after the baby, but with her energy there was no way she was going to live permanently in the country doing nothing. In fact, she did a lot of Churchill's entertaining. She 'lived' in Downing Street and Chequers and formed the Churchill Club for servicemen, and I used to go there as a soldier. She shared a flat with Kathy, Harriman's daughter, at 49 Grosvenor Square.

Anita Leslie reveals in *Cousin Randolph* that Pamela made it clear to him she intended divorce. The bombing had eased and she removed half the furniture from the marital home in Hertfordshire to the Grosvenor Square flat in London where she was now living with two-year-old Winston and his nanny. 'There she entertained generals, diplomats, journalists and socialites with great flair and dinners that included ingredients practically unobtainable in ration-struck Britain,' says Ogden.

American uniforms were becoming a familiar sight in the battered London streets in 1943, and Pamela gave up her ministry job to act as co-hostess at the Churchill Club, which opened as a cultural refuge for American and Allied servicemen. Top army men and Hollywood stars in the forces were among the audiences at music, art and poetry evenings, and Ogden suggests that Pamela was more than friendly with some of them.

After Averell's despatch to Moscow as the US Ambassador to Russia, Pamela found consolation for his absence in the arms of American commentator Ed Murrow, whose memorable broadcasts to his own country during the London blitz were of considerable propaganda value to an embattled Britain. He will also be remembered for his post-war interview and exposé on television that helped bring down the notorious demagogue, Senator Joseph McCarthy, during the anti-Communist witch-hunts in America. Although politically at the opposite end of the class spectrum from Pamela - Murrow was the left wing son of a humble timber worker as well as twelve years her senior - they planned to get married, but after the war he jilted her in favour of his Swedish wife and child.

Randolph gave Pamela the grounds for the 1946 divorce by walking out after their row, and she escaped from the depression of war-weary Britain to mix with the sophisticated hedonists of unscathed Paris, the French Riviera and St Moritz.

She made the acquaintance of Aly Khan, the pleasure-loving son of the religious leader and wealthy racehorse owner Aga Khan, and joined Aly at his luxury villa near Cannes on the French Riviera, where he introduced her to the playboy amoureux, among them Gianni Agnelli, the handsome twenty-seven year old heir to the Italian car manufacturer Fiat. She shared her time between the flat he bought her in Paris, complete with car and chauffeur, and his villas in the south of France, where she looked after his guests with the attentive care to detail that came naturally to her. There is a story that after Pamela discovered Agnelli in bed with another woman, he fled in such haste that he crashed his Ferrari into the back of a lorry, car or horse-and-cart - accounts differ. All the same, marriage seemed in prospect, and she converted to Roman Catholicism, but the philandering Agnelli chose instead an Italian princess who was pregnant by him. Wiping away her tears, Pamela succumbed to the attentions of Elie de Rothschild, the married son of the banker and vineyard owner Elie de Rothschild senior, who headed one of the most celebrated and richest families in Europe. They enjoyed six years together, horse-riding, travelling, sailing the Mediterranean, mixing with the diplomatic and social elite of Europe, but even though Pamela was socially acquainted with the Duke and Duchess of Windsor, she was not invited to the British Embassy reception for Queen Elizabeth during her visit to Paris in 1957. According to Ogden, the ambassador's wife was adamant, 'I will not have that tart in this embassy!'

Pamela had long been attracted by the Americans and their way of life, and when Leland Hayward proposed to divorce his latest wife, she migrated to New York where he was producing the Broadway hit *Gypsy*, starring Ethel Merriman, while negotiating for the rights to *The Sound of Music*. He had already produced a string of hits, from *South Pacific* to *Call me Madam* and movie versions of Hemingway's short story *The Old Man of the Sea*, with Spencer Tracy, and *The Spirit of St Louis*, starring James Stewart. He finally obtained his divorce from his third wife, and in May 1959 he and Pamela flew to matrimony in Carson City, Nevada. He was fifty-nine and she twenty years younger. By now a wealthy woman, she bought a lavish apartment in New York's Fifth Avenue and later a house in fifty-seven wooded acres of Westchester County, only eighteen helicopter minutes from the city. By the late 1960s the appetites of the theatre-going public were changing, the final curtain began to drop on Leland's phenomenal career, and like a tragic scene from one of his own productions he took to his sick bed. Pamela nursed him with tender affection to the end in 1971.

Her brother Edward, now Lord Digby since the death of their father in 1964, flew to America and presided at the reading of the will which left half of Hayward's possessions to Pamela and the remainder to his son, Bill, and daughter, Brooke, who were the children of his previous marriage to the actress Margaret Sullivan. The atmosphere in the Westchester sitting-room was strained. Ogden describes the relationship between Brooke and Pamela as 'a classic case of a talented headstrong daughter clashing with a determined, self-centred stepmother in a battle of wills for a father/husband's love and favour.' The tense meeting had to break up because the mourners were arriving, among them Frank Sinatra and Jacqueline Onassis.

Edward said:

> I liked Leland very much. He was the first person to break the reign of the movie moguls in the 1920s as an independent producer. He was an agent for talented people and managed to pump up their salaries on Broadway. He combined a big heart with toughness. At his funeral James Stewart and all the stars were there and a lot of minor actors, and several said, 'When I was down he slipped me a $100'. He was a very kind man.

Six months later Pamela married her wartime lover, Averell Harriman, who had lost his wife twelve months before, thus fostering the allegations that no sooner had one liaison died than she started another liaison with someone else. Edward discounts the slur on her reputation:

> I know exactly what happened; I was with her when Leland died. She came over to England very miserable and wondering whether to move back to here. She looked after Leland very well indeed, but she was very unhappy. When she went back to New York a friend said, 'Oh, you're coming to a party in Washington this evening', and she said 'Oh, don't be ridiculous, I can't do that'. The friend replied, 'It's all arranged,' and they flew to Washington. At the party Averell said to Pamela: 'Now you're going to marry me.'

Like her previous two husbands, he had visited Minterne House, and he stayed there two or three times. He was eighty, nearly thirty years older than his new bride and growing deaf, but Pamela enabled the elder statesman of the Democratic Party to continue his political life and meetings through her. She entertained his many visitors and transformed his magnificent house in Georgetown, a select district of Washington, with the taste for beautiful and artistic things she had acquired during her residence in Paris. She seems not have neglected her ancestral roots or the cachet which the English peerage carries in the States. The Digby coat of arms with the Latin motto *Deo Non Fortuna* (From God not Fortune) appeared everywhere in the décor; on pillows, and even on stationery and matchboxes and on a silver ostrich Edward gave her to replace the Mercedes star on her car.

He does not know how the ostrich with a horseshoe in its mouth became attached to the Digbys, but believes the origin may have been an ancient legend telling how a Roman legion in North Africa was defeated in battle because its cavalry was outflanked by boys on fast-moving ostriches which terrified the invaders' horses, hence the horseshoe. The two monkeys supporting the ostrich can be traced to an incident in 1495 when Kildare Castle, the seat of the ancient Irish family of

Fitzgerald, caught fire, and the son and heir of the Earl of Kildare was trapped in a turret with a pet monkey. 'Suddenly out of the window came the monkey with the baby safely in its arms – and I wouldn't be here if it wasn't for that monkey,' smiled Edward. One of his ancestors, Sir Robert Digby, married Lettice Lady Othaly, the Heir General of the Earl of Kildare, a marriage that explains why monkeys joined the ostrich to become the menagerie on the Digby crest. Robert was created an Irish peer in 1620, and in 1765 a descendant was admitted to the British nobility.

Perhaps the lesson of this story, the importance of beating the competition with agile tactics and a beakful of luck, inspired the adventurous Digby clan, and Pamela was certainly intrigued by the romantic adventures of a nineteenth-century forebear, Jane Digby, who married at nineteen, deserted her much older husband and eminent lawyer Lord Ellenborough, had two illegitimate children by German Prince Schwarzenberg, and after other liaisons moved smartly through the courts of King Ludwig of Bavaria and his son Otho, King of Greece, conquering their sovereign hearts on the way. She finally wed a Syrian sheikh on condition that he abandoned his harem.

Pamela had taken American citizenship and threw herself into the politics of her adopted country on the strength of her ageing husband's lingering party clout. To aid the Democrats' forthcoming fights in federal, state and local elections she formed a powerful action group, Democrats for the Eighties, with herself as Chairman, aimed at stemming the party's ebbing morale, modernising the party organisation, and raising millions of dollars, not a little of it Harriman's. She redoubled her efforts after his death in 1986 at the age of ninety-five, and flew to meetings and conferences all over the country in the executive jet he had bought her.

With her reputation as a 'hostess with the mostest', she entertained the well-heeled glitterati to sumptuous dinners and other wallet-fingering get-togethers in the Georgetown mansion, and $12 million tipped into the party's coffers helped fund the election of Clinton in 1992. The end of the Republican presence in the White House was a triumph for her determination. This success was to be consummated by Clinton's re-election to the Presidency four years later, and he rewarded his friend with the juiciest plum on the US diplomatic circuit, the embassy in Paris.

At her formal nomination before the Senate Foreign Relations Committee, Senator Charles Robb praised her 'obvious wit, charm, intellect and grace' and 'almost everything she has done throughout her very distinguished career has managed to play an important role and indeed help to shape events'. Pamela replied, 'I come before you today conscious of one great difference between us and one great similarity. Unlike you, I was not born in this country – I am an American by choice – but like all of you I have a deep love for this land that has long been my home, and I am proud to serve it in any way I can.' The full senate approved the appointment unanimously.

Nevertheless, critical eyebrows were raised about the extent of her hands-on experience in government and, above all, her age, but cosmetic surgery lifted twenty years from her seventy-two, and with her stylish champagne-tinted hair she looked gorgeous, and she was fluent in French. In fact, she had extensive knowledge of foreign affairs, having travelled widely with globe-trotting Harriman and had discussions with important leaders in many countries. During the Russian President's visit to Washington, she invited Raisa Gorbachev to meet eminent women at her Georgetown home. To gauge the width of her interests, in the early 1990s she was serving on no less than fourteen political and cultural committees and organisations, including the English-speaking Union of the United States (as Vice-President) and the Winston Churchill Foundation of the US (as a trustee). Edward notes:

> If you look at her career right through it would be reasonable to say that all her experiences trained her for a diplomatic job. She learned from each liaison. It was an American tradition to have non-professionals as ambassadors. What was remarkable was the absolute loyalty and devotion to her in Paris; she was able to carry her staff with her, and that is very important. In that situation there could have been a lot of jealousy and back-stabbing.

Dealing tactfully with trade, defence, finance and other tricky questions in Paris, she showed mastery of her new calling, and the French took a tolerant and amused view of her reported *scandales de cœur*. She proved to be a skilful mediator during those difficult periods that recur in Franco-American relations. There were differences, for instance, over the GATT agreement on free trade and on intervention in Bosnia, but being on close terms with the presidents of two very different cultures, she was able to get them to talk to each other. Edward regards this feat as her greatest achievement.

At home in America, the picture was not so rosy. She could not escape her past, and there were disputes with stepchildren. Leland Hayward's will had led to suspicions and recriminations on the part of the Margaret Sullivan children, Bill and Brooke, and now Harriman's offspring felt aggrieved at the large bequests to Pamela of property, pictures and a fortune of at least $66 million. The generous nature of the bequests reflected the genuine love Averell and she had shared, and Pamela had been a fond and caring wife in his final years of deafness and disability. He himself had said, 'The happiest years of my life have been with Pam.'

His children accepted the will which left $30 million in trust for his grandchildren, but an allegation arose that she had misused the fund, and the bitter wrangle ended only when she settled $11 million on them. Even after paying the enormous legal costs of the action, she still had millions in the bank to ease her old age.

The extent of her wealth was revealed in her own will, which showed that she had left $10 million to her own son Winston, then a Conservative Member of Parliament. According to Gary Younge in *The Guardian*, he could have inherited at least fifteen times as much had his mother not lost a fortune in her legal battles and unwise investments. The only person mentioned in the will, apart from Winston and his wife, was her brother Edward. 'I was left money, but it was for Minterne,' he said. 'She was always very keen that Minterne House should be kept going.' Her only charitable gift was her most precious possession, a Van Gogh painting which went to the National Gallery of Art in Washington. An auction of her effects – furniture, paintings, and historic items – well-exceeded the estimate and raised $4.6 million, of which $1.4 million came from the sale of John Singer Sargent's

Staircase in Capri and $184,000 from *Jug with Bottles*, painted by her father-in-law Winston Churchill. The President of Sotheby's, Diana Brooks, said before the auction that Pamela's collection reflected her 'refined taste and flair', and the letters, photographs and books and other personal memorabilia 'offered a fascinating glimpse into the life of one of the most accomplished women of our era'.

Although Pamela became a multi-millionairess, Edward feels there has been too much emphasis on her pursuit of wealth. 'She was not looking for money,' he said. 'She had always been more attracted to people with power rather than money. They do not always go together, but they are inclined to. She liked people older than herself because they were interesting.' He discounted the suggestion that Prime Minister Churchill put her on to the Harriman relationship:

> It was more Harriman seducing her than her seducing Harriman. I think he was always the great love of her life. He refused to marry her and would not divorce his wife. She was good at looking after men, but she did not move from man to man. It was they who would not marry her. She was loyal to whoever was the man of the time. I think none of these men would themselves agree to the innuendoes in Ogden's book.

The fatal collapse after her regular swim in the Ritz Hotel pool close to the embassy was all the more unexpected because, as Edward said:

> She had always kept herself fit, doing a lot of walking, and her passion for riding had never left her. She had a house in Virginia (at Middleburgh) which was like pre-war Dorset, people in bowler hats and top hats, women riding side-saddle, and that sort of thing, and she had a lot of show jumpers. On her last weekend at Minterne she climbed High Stoy (a local hill) and walked us all off our feet.

Winston was sitting beside her hospital bed at Neuilly-sur-Seine when she died without regaining consciousness from the collapse the previous day.

At a valedictory assembly on the embassy lawn, French President Jacques Chirac said:

> Today France loses a friend. All those gathered here who loved her and loved working with her feel great sorrow. My wife and I share their grief and distress. President Clinton and the American people must be aware of the great respect and regard which were felt for her here in France.

Chirac then revealed:

> A month ago in my office I told her of my intention to bestow upon her, at the end of her term as ambassador, the highest of our honours. It is my regret that the ceremony has become today a last leave-taking.

Reverentially, Chirac placed on the US flag draped over the coffin a purple cushion bearing the scarlet sash and gold medal of the Grand Cross of the Legion of

Honour. The English girl from rural Dorset had become the first American woman to receive France's highest honour.

Edward and Winston were in the motorcade that carried Pamela to the airport where, in cold but bright sunshine, France paid its final tribute with a fifty-strong ceremonial guard of honour and a military band. 'There was a lot of marching, rather like our trooping of the colour,' Edward recalled. An American guard of honour escorted the coffin along a red carpet to the US Presidential jet. Winston accompanied his mother's body to Washington and a greeting in freezing snow from a military escort and Secretary of State Madeleine Albright. 'We are here,' she declared, 'to welcome home a great American hero.'

What will history make of Dorset's most famous woman, a glamorous legend in her time, who rests in the Harriman cemetery at his home, Arden House, in New York State? Will it remember her, as some commentators allege, as a courtesan who used her womanly charms in an unscrupulous pursuit of wealth and power? Or will it be as the President of the United States described her in a letter to Edward and Dione on White House notepaper when the Digby family returned from attending the funeral:

> I'm glad we were able to find a moment to talk last weekend before our final tribute to Pamela Harriman. Although words alone will never suffice to describe the breadth and grandeur of her life and accomplishments, I hope that together we succeeded in remembering this remarkable woman as befits her legacy - with eloquence and grace.
> Sincerely,
> Bill Clinton.

Views from the Top

Few American citizens can have been the object of such fulsome eulogies from the government heads of the US and France. President Jacques Chirac, in his farewell address in the Paris embassy garden, said:

> Today the United States' oldest ally mourns the death of a great ambassador. Two centuries ago Benjamin Franklin and then Thomas Jefferson represented in Paris a nascent America. In 1993 President Bill Clinton chose an exceptional person to follow in their footsteps. Pamela Harriman symbolised the indissoluble ties between the Old World and the New, the transatlantic community for which she did so much. She personified England through her birth into the British aristocracy and her marriage to the son of Sir Winston Churchill. At his side she shared in the sacrifices made by the British people so that freedom might survive.
>
> Before the war she had chosen to stay in France at the Sorbonne, and then after the Liberation she came here again to begin working as a journalist (on the social diary of *The London Evening Standard* owned by Lord Beaverbrooke). She was here to see France rise again to its feet, thanks in particular to the Marshall Plan, the fiftieth anniversary of which we will be commemorating in a few weeks' time.

In 1959 she left Europe for the United States. It was then, when she crossed the Atlantic and met the future President Kennedy that her political commitment began. Her commitment was unremitting. For three decades Pamela Churchill Hayward, who became Pamela Harriman, was an inspiration to the Democratic Party, devoting all her energy to it through thick and thin. In 1980 she recognised in the young Governor of Arkansas, Bill Clinton, one of the future leaders of her party. She became his lasting friend. In 1992 she gave him decisive support, and when the new president had to choose that man or women who could best personify French-American friendship in Paris he thought, discerningly, of Pamela Harriman.

To say that she was an exceptional representative of the United States in France does not do justice to her achievement. She lent to our long-standing alliance the radiant strength of her personality. She was elegance itself, she was grace, she vested in our friendship her deep affection for the French people and her unique familiarity with our country and its culture, old and new.

This great lady was also a peerless diplomat. In the impassioned debates which are a regular feature of the friendship between our two countries she was for both President Clinton and myself an indispensable participant, heeding the thoughts, reading the expectations and constraints of each, conveying these faithfully as always. At our many meetings she often found the way forward to agreement. She did this with her unfailing intelligence, charm, generosity and insight.

President Clinton was no less generous in his praise of his friend at the funeral service in Washington's neo-Gothic National Cathedral on 13 February 1997, which was attended by members of the Digby family and a congregation of the distinguished in many fields. In his eulogy he said:

We gather in tribute to Pamela Harriman, patriot and public servant, American ambassador and citizen of the world, mother, grandmother, great-grandmother and sister and, for so many of us here, a cherished friend. She adopted our country with extraordinary devotion. Today her country bids her farewell with profound gratitude. Hillary (his wife) and I have often talked about what made Pamela so remarkable. It was more than her elegance, as unforgettable as that was. It was more than the lilt of her voice and her laughter, more even than the luminous presence that could light up a room, a convention hall or even the City of Light itself. It was more than her vibrant sense of history and the wisdom that came to her from the great events she had lived through and those she had helped to shape, from the Battle of Britain to the peace accord in Bosnia.

I think it was most of all that she was truly indomitable. One day the train she was on to London was bombed twice during the Blitz. She simply brushed off the shards of glass, picked herself up, and went to the office to do her work at the Ministry of Supply. She was twenty-one years old. More than forty years later all of us who knew her saw the same resolve and strength again and again, most tenderly in the way she gave not only love but dignity and pride to Averell who, as long as he was with her, was at the summit even to his last days.

In 1991 she put her indomitability to a new test in American politics, forming an organisation with a name that made the pundits chuckle because it did seem a laughable oxymoron in those days: Democrats for the Eighties. For members of our party at that low ebb she became organiser, inspirer, sustainer, a captain of our cause, in a long march back to victory. She lifted our spirits and our vision. I will never forget how she was there for Hillary and for me in 1992 – wise counsel, friend, a leader in our ranks who never doubted the outcome or, if she did, covered it so well with her well known bravado that no-one could have suspected.

Today I am here in no small measure because she was there. She was one of the easiest choices I made for any appointment when I became President. As she left to become our ambassador to France she told us all with a smile 'Now my home in Paris will be your home. Please come and visit us – but not all at once.' It seemed she had been having us at her home all at once for too many years, so a lot of us took her up on her invitation to come to Paris. After Hillary and I had been there the first time I must say I wondered which one of us got the better job.

In many ways her whole life was a preparation for these last four years of singular service and achievement. She represented America with wisdom, grace and dignity, earning the confidence of France's leaders, the respect of its people, the devotion of her staff. Born a European – and American by choice, as she liked to say – Pamela worked hard to build the very strongest ties between our two countries and continents. She understood that to make yourself heard you had to know how to listen, and with the special appreciation of one not native-born she felt to her bones America's special leadership role in the world.

Today we see her legacy in the growing promise of Europe undivided, secure and free, a legacy that moved President Chirac last week to confer upon Pamela the Grand Cross of the Legion of Honour, France's highest award. He said then that seldom since Benjamin Franklin and Thomas Jefferson had America been so well served in France. There is one image of Pamela Harriman I will always treasure. I can see her now, standing on the windswept beaches of Normandy on the fiftieth anniversary of D-Day. She had told many of us of the long, tense night in England half a century before as they waited for news about the transports ploughing towards the shore, filled with young soldiers – American, British and Free French. Now, fifty years later, history had come full circle, and she was there as an active life-force in the greatest continuing alliance for freedom the world has ever known.

I was so glad that Randolph read a few moments ago from the book of Sir Winston Churchill's essays that Pamela loved so well and gave to so many of us who were her friends. The passage he read not only describes her own life, it is her valediction to us, her final instruction about how we should live our lives, and I think she would like this service to be not only grand, as it is, but to be a final instruction from her to us about what we should now do. Let me quote just a portion of what was said a few moments ago: 'Let us reconcile ourselves to the mysterious rhythm of our destinies such as they must be in this world of time and space. Let us treasure our joys but not bewail our sorrows. The glory of light cannot exist without the shadows. Life is a whole, and the journey has been well worth making.'

Throughout her glorious journey Pamela Harriman lightened the shadows of our lives. Now she is gone. In the mysterious rhythm of her destiny she left at the pinnacle of her public service with the promise of her beloved America burning brighter because of how she lived in her space and time. What a journey it was, and well worth making. May God comfort her family and countless friends, and may He keep her soul indomitable forever.

Those words, coming from the most powerful man in the world at that time, are convincing testimony that Pamela Churchill Hayward Harriman, née Digby, is Dorset's most famous feminine link with North America.

Index

CL

Numbers preceded by 'C' refer to colour images.

Visit our website and discover thousands of other History Press books.
www.thehistorypress.co.uk